"Scripture speaks of 'the unsearchable riches of Christ' (Ephesians 3:8). In *Rich Wounds*, David takes us into these endless riches with his beautiful reflections on the Savior. A deeply edifying book."

DANE ORTLUND, Author, *Gentle and Lowly*

"Weaving together biblical truth, historical treasures mined from hymns, and contemporary challenging insights, Mathis has produced a masterpiece guaranteed to refresh even the most stagnant heart. Reading these short, simple yet deeply profound reflections, I was compelled to put down Mathis's book, open my Bible, and worship."

LINDA ALLCOCK, Author, *Head, Heart, Hands* and *Deeper Still*

"David Mathis takes one treasure at a time, drawn from the life, death, resurrection, and exaltation of Jesus, and reverently unpacks it and meditates on it. This book is well-written and edifying."

D.A. CARSON, Emeritus Professor of New Testament,
Trinity Evangelical Divinity School

"There's nothing I find more meaningful or satisfying to contemplate than Jesus himself. In *Rich Wounds*, David Mathis has written a warm, concise, and celebratory treatment of the Jesus who is everything we need and—may God use this book to help us realize this—everything we want."

RANDY ALCORN, Author, *It's All about Jesus*

"More than anything else in these troubled and troubling times, our souls need a fresh look at our Savior. *Rich Wounds* will help you drink deeply from the fountain of Christ's love and discover in him life-giving pools of grace. Thirty days of savoring him and meditating on the griefs he bore on your behalf will be a sweet balm for your heart and will lead you to springs of deepest joy."

NANCY DEMOSS WOLGEMUTH, Founder, Revive Our Hearts

"David Mathis has a keen ability to unpack theological truths with striking clarity. His gifting is on full display in *Rich Wounds* as he guides us through the life, sacrifice, and glorification of our Savior in reflections that are both poignant and profound. As Mathis directs our gaze to the person of Christ, the heart cannot help but stir with adoration and praise for the Son, who suffered wounds so that ours might be healed. Read this devotional slowly, and delight in the one who makes all things new."

KATHRYN BUTLER, MD, Author, *Between Life and Death*

"Martin Luther famously said, 'To progress in the Christian life is to begin again.' *Rich Wounds* will help you begin again and again by taking you deeply into the surrender, suffering, and exaltation of Jesus. It is filled with profound insight and will help you not just understand but also feel the weight of Jesus' atoning work."

J.D. GREEAR, Pastor, The Summit Church, Raleigh-Durham, NC; Author, *Just Ask*

"This book is a treasure trove of fresh biblical insights, deep devotion, and practical help. Each of its thirty chapters is engaging, moving, and perceptive, with useful prayers and Bible readings to help you immerse yourself in God's love and compassion in Christ. This book will help you meditate more deeply on the 'rich wounds' of the Lord Jesus Christ, our Saviour: his humanity, life, ministry, death, and resurrection and glorification."

PETER ADAM, Former principal, Ridley College, Melbourne, Australia

"This volume sings with an infectious enthusiasm of the Christ whose rich wounds are worthy of many crowns. Written in an accessible style, it moves from the wonder of God's love displayed on the cross to the stunning eruption of his power in the resurrection, when joy triumphed over sorrow. *Rich Wounds* will help us sing as we think, and think as we sing."

DONALD MACLEOD, Former principal, Free Church of Scotland College

"Let David draw your eyes away from yourself and on to the rich wounds of Christ—the only wounds that heal."

ABIGAIL DODDS, Blogger; Author, *(A)Typical Woman*

"I have been nourished by many devotional books, but normally as a spiritual appetizer—an energy-booster—for the day. Mathis' devotions are more like bite-sized meals. They are chock-full of robust theology and scriptural depth, feeding my soul with the glory of Jesus. The title is fitting: we feed from and are quickly sated by the wounds of Christ on each page."

MATT REAGAN, Director, Campus Outreach Charleston

RICH
WOUNDS

The Countless Treasures of the
Life, Death, and Triumph of Jesus

DAVID MATHIS

thegoodbook
COMPANY

Rich Wounds
© David C. Mathis, 2022

Published by:
The Good Book Company

thegoodbook.com | thegoodbook.co.uk
thegoodbook.com.au | thegoodbook.co.nz | thegoodbook.co.in

ISBN: 9781784986841 | Printed in Turkey

Cover design by Faceout Studio

To Mercy

CONTENTS

INTRODUCTION

The Many Crowns of Christ

"His eyes are like a flame of fire,
and on his head are many diadems."
–Revelation 19:12

Admiration may be the highest of pleasures, and particularly when we marvel at the life, death, and triumph of Jesus. The treasures of who he is, what he has done, and what he will do are countless. We were made for this: not just to trust and obey God, but to know him, and enjoy him, in Jesus. The joys of knowing Jesus are unsurpassed even now—and they will endure, and only deepen and develop, for all eternity to come.

This Jesus is a king unlike any other. Mere human monarchs and dignitaries have their strengths and weaknesses, their fortes and flaws, the particular glories for which they are remembered and the inevitable missteps they wish to be forgotten. Yet the man Christ Jesus—not only truly human but also truly God—eclipses and far surpasses every other human ruler and celebrity. He is worthy of more than a single crown. As King of kings, and Lord of lords, and Glory of glories, he is worthy of many crowns.

Because of how it helps me admire and marvel at Jesus, one of my favorite hymns has long been "Crown Him with Many Crowns" (Matthew Bridges, 1851). In my own life, it's one of the few hymns that has been a common thread from one church to another. I have been singing it for forty years, since I was a child, then in college, then as an adult. Now, my kids know I love it and get my attention when the first bars begin in church. "Dad, it's your favorite!"

Over the years, in singing this hymn with congregation after congregation, I've often been moved to tears of joy as I have pondered, even just vaguely, the great coronation ceremony in heaven, where the risen Christ, always fully God and now in full glorified humanity, takes his seat on the throne of the universe. I love how the hymn's stanzas celebrate Christ, in turn, as Lord of love, Lord of life, Lord of light, Lord of heaven, Lord of years, Lord of lords. Even as phrase after phrase tells of his glory, the one that has arrested me most over the years is "rich wounds."

> *Crown him the Lord of love!*
>   *Behold his hands and side—*
> *Rich wounds, yet visible above,*
>   *In beauty glorified.*

Rich wounds captures so well the strangeness and beauty— the peculiar glory—of Jesus Christ and his self-sacrifice at the cross for sinners. "Wounds," of course, is no foreign word to modern ears. Today we speak with surprising frequency about "wounds:" not so much physical wounds as the emotional ones we're newly aware of and attend to— the "daddy wound" of fatherlessness, the "wound" of harsh words against us, the "wounds" of some trauma that continues to haunt us. As a society, we've become freshly conscious of our wounds. We talk about them. We know them.

But here we celebrate *rich wounds*. Jesus was wounded for us: pierced for our transgressions, crushed for our iniquities. "Upon him was the chastisement that brought us peace, and with his wounds we are healed" (Isaiah 53:5). Jesus bore *our* griefs, *our* sorrows, *our* transgressions, *our* iniquities; he brought *us* peace; he healed *us*.

His wounds, horrific as they were when inflicted on the innocent Son of God, are indeed *rich* wounds, because he is God, and made us rich in becoming poor for us (2 Corinthians 8:9). They are wounds rich in meaning and significance: wounds that have not vanished on his resurrected body. They are still visible—gloriously so, as the hymn tells us, and as we'll celebrate in this book, especially in chapter 22.

"Rich wounds" flies as a banner over Jesus' life and death and new life in the resurrection. First came his ability to be wounded, which he embraced by virtue of his becoming man and taking human flesh; then of course came the hand and foot and side wounds he endured in his death; and then, most significantly, came the scars which he now displays on his glorified body, celebrated in the hymn. "Rich wounds" not only brings to mind the cross and his death, not only the life and words and works that led him there, but also his resurrection: his exaltation to God's right hand, his coronation as King of the universe, and his reign in heaven now. And "rich wounds" speaks to Christ's ability to transform our wounds today, like his, into marks of beauty—wounds which are not without their pain, nor without subsequent glory.

The thirty chapters in this book are meditations on the many crowns—the many glories—of Jesus Christ, and in particular his redemptive work for his people in his life, sacrificial death, and world-turning resurrection.

Part 1 considers eight glimpses of his glory in his life and ministry, leading up to his Passion week. Then Part 2 pauses to consider his sacrificial death on the cross and its meaning for his people. Part 3 lingers in a place from which we can be prone to move on too quickly: his resurrection.

Many of us do make much of his resurrection—for one day each year. One aspect of this book that excites me most is this opportunity for abiding, pausing, remaining in the glory of the resurrection, which was so prominent in the early preaching of the apostles, yet can at times occupy a relatively small space in our own preaching and theology. Finally, in Part 4, I invite you to walk with me, as we walk with Jesus through his Passion week (often called "Holy Week")—from Palm Sunday, to Good Friday, to Resurrection Sunday.

Over the years, my church and family have enjoyed recovering the ancient traditions of Advent, Lent, and Holy Week—celebrating these seasons with special meditations to draw our hearts afresh to the glory of Christ. I hope the chapters in this book will serve in this way for some, as devotions for the month leading up to Easter. Certainly, Part 4, which maps onto the eight days of Holy Week, may be particularly helpful then. I have included a passage of Scripture to read alongside each chapter for those who wish to pair it with daily Bible reading. But this book is not only for Lent. I hope that it will feed readers year-round—since we always have need of considering Christ Jesus, made flesh, crucified, risen, and exalted.

I love meditating on the many glories, the many crowns, the many wonders and excellencies of Jesus Christ. Ponder with me his life and ministry, his sacrificial death, his spectacular resurrection, and that one fateful week that was the worst and most wonderful in the history of the world.

Part 1

HIS LIFE

"He has done all things well."
—Mark 7:37

David Mathis

hearing" (Luke 4:21). Jesus ide
"he of whom it is written" (M
he cleared the temple of
what is written in Isaia
Luke 19:46). He
(Mark 7:6; Lu
vary, he kn
(see espe
16; 15
he

an

We m
al spiritual practices in the Gospels, but what we do
have is no accident, nor is it scant. We know exactly what
God means for us to know, in just the right detail—and we
have far more about Jesus' personal spiritual rhythms than
we do about anyone else in the Bible.

Quiet Times without a Bible

First, observe the place of Scripture in Jesus' life. He did
not have his own personal material copy of the Bible, like
almost all of us do today. He heard what was read aloud in
the synagogue, and what his mother sang, and he rehearsed
what he had put to memory. And yet throughout his record-
ed ministry we see evidence of a man utterly captivated by
what is written in the text of Scripture.

At the very outset of his public ministry, Jesus retreated
to the wilderness; there, as he was tempted by the devil, he
leaned on *what is written* (Matthew 4:4, 6, 7, 10; Luke 4:4,
8, 10). Then, returning to his hometown of Nazareth, he
stood up to read, took the scroll of Isaiah (61:1-2), and announced, "Today this Scripture has been fulfilled in your

ntified John the Baptist as
atthew 11:10; Luke 7:27), and
oneychangers on the grounds of
56:7 (Matthew 21:13; Mark 11:17;
buked the proud by quoting Scripture
20:17). At every step of the way to Cal-
w everything would happen "as it is written"
ially John's Gospel: 6:31, 45; 8:17; 10:34; 12:14,
:25). "The Son of Man goes as it is written of him,"
said (Mark 14:21). "See, we are going up to Jerusalem,
and everything that is written about the Son of Man by the
prophets will be accomplished" (Luke 18:31).

Let there be no confusion about the central place of God's
written word in Jesus' life. He lived by what was written.

How Often He Withdrew

For Christ, "the wilderness" or "desolate place" often became
his momentarily sacred space. He regularly escaped the noise
and frenzy of society to be alone with his Father, giving him
his full attention.

After "his fame spread everywhere" (Mark 1:28) and "the
whole city was gathered together at the door" (v 33), Jesus
took a remarkable step:

> *"Rising very early in the morning, while it was still
> dark, he departed and went out to a desolate place,
> and there he prayed." (v 35)*

What a ministry opportunity he left behind, some might
think. Surely some of us would have skipped or shortened
our private spiritual habits to hurry off and bless the swell-
ing masses. To be sure, other times would come when Jesus
would delay his personal routines to meet immediate needs.
But how many of us, in such a situation, would have the

presence of mind—and the heart—to discern our need and prioritize prayer as Jesus did?

Luke also shows unmistakably that this pattern of retreat and re-entry was part of the ongoing dynamic of Christ's human life. Jesus "departed and went into a desolate place" (Luke 4:42)—not just once but regularly. "He would withdraw to desolate places and pray" (5:16).

So also in Matthew. After the death of John the Baptist, Jesus "withdrew from there in a boat to a desolate place by himself" (Matthew 14:13). Even then, the crowds pursued him. Yet he didn't despise them—here he puts his desire to retreat on hold—but had compassion on them and healed their sick (v 14). After feeding them, a crowd five thousand strong, he withdrew again to a quiet place. "After he had dismissed the crowds, he went up on the mountain by himself to pray" (v 23).

Praying Alone and Together

What is written animated his life, and when he withdrew, he went to speak to his Father in prayer. At times, he went away *by himself*, to be *alone* (Matthew 14:23; Mark 6:46-47). "He went out to the mountain *to pray*, and all night he continued *in prayer* to God" (Luke 6:12).

He also prayed with others. The disciples saw him model prayer at his baptism (Luke 3:21), as he laid his hands on the children (Matthew 19:13), and when he drove out demons (Mark 9:29). He prayed with his disciples; even when he prayed alone, they were sometimes at hand (Luke 9:18; also 11:1). He took Peter, John, and James "and went up on the mountain to pray" (9:28). On the night before he died, he said to Peter, "I have *prayed for you* that your faith may not fail" (22:32). All of John 17 is his prayer for his disciples, in the hearing of the Twelve, minus Judas. Then they went out from that upper room and saw him pray over and over in the garden (Matthew 26:36, 39, 42, 44). He not only modeled prayer but instructed them in how to pray. "Pray then like this…" (6:9-13).

Come Away with Me

Jesus didn't only retreat to be alone with God but also *invited* his disciples to join him. In Mark 6:31-32, he tells them, "Come away by yourselves to a desolate place and rest a while." Mark explains, "For many were coming and going, and they had no leisure even to eat. And they went away in the boat to a desolate place by themselves." So also, in the Gospel of John, as his fame spread, Jesus retreated from more populated settings to invest in his disciples in more desolate, less distracting places (John 11:54).

And this is his invitation to us, as well, today: to cultivate habits of withdrawing to hear from God and respond in prayer, and then of returning, with our hearts and minds renewed, to echo the heart of Christ in acts of love toward those he has put along our path. This is my prayer for you as we linger over the glories of Christ in the chapters of this book: that your soul would be fed and formed in quiet moments, meditating on his word, and that you would be newly energized in the callings he has given you.

In it all—in receiving his Father's voice in Scripture and in praying alone (and with company)—Jesus sought communion with his Father. His habits were not demonstrations of raw will and sheer discipline. His acts of receiving the word and responding in prayer were not ends in themselves. In these blessed *means*, he pursued the *end* of communing with his Father.

—

Father, in our hurried and distracting times, grant that we would be more like your Son—that we would not rush off incessantly to the next to-do, but that we would give our first and best energy to communing with you, hearing your voice in your word, and enjoying the gift of having your ear in prayer. Against the grain of our day, strengthen us to come away and retreat to meet with you, and in grace send us back to engage with our needy world, with our hunger first met in Christ. In his name we pray. Amen.

Scripture reading: Matthew 14:13-23

2. HIS PURPOSE

Why Jesus Lived

*"For this purpose
I have come to this hour.
Father, glorify your name."
–John 12:27-28*

No one lived quite like Jesus. Ordinary as he looked, and was in many ways—with "no form or majesty" (Isaiah 53:2) to turn heads—his earthly life as a whole surpassed every other human life, not only those of his contemporaries but of all others before and since. In the final tally, Jesus stands alone. No other human has left such a deep and enduring impression on the world, and he did this in only three years of active public life.

He turned water into wine. He multiplied loaves and fish. He gave sight to the blind. He even raised the dead. But he also taught with a peculiar, unmatched authority. His words carried weight like those of no other human voice. "They were astonished at his teaching" (Mark 1:22). "All the people were hanging on his words" (Luke 19:48). Even those who opposed him had to recognize that "No one ever spoke like this man!" (John 7:46). And still today we marvel at his words.

What was it that drove such a life and such timeless teaching? *Why* did Jesus live? What got him up in the morning and motivated him to open his mouth, even under great opposition? What was *the goal*—and, in the end, *the effect*—of his life, so far as we can discern?

The Effect of His Life

No wonder that the angels declared, "Glory to God!" in announcing his birth (Luke 2:14). As Jesus began to teach and minister publicly, the reported effect, again and again, was not that the people praised *him*, but that they glorified *God*.

He healed the paralysed man, who "rose and immediately picked up his bed and went out before them all, so that they were all amazed and *glorified God*" (Mark 2:12). As Matthew tells it, "When the crowds saw it, they were afraid, and *they glorified God*, who had given such authority to men" (Matthew 9:8). Luke makes explicit that it was both the healed paralytic who glorified God (Luke 5:25) and the crowd (v 26).

In fact, *glorifying God* is Matthew's summary of the effect of all Jesus' miracle-working: "The crowd wondered, when they saw the mute speaking, the crippled healthy, the lame walking, and the blind seeing. And they *glorified the God of Israel*" (Matthew 15:31). And when Jesus restored sight to a blind beggar, Luke tells us that both the man and the crowd directed their praises to God: "Immediately he recovered his sight and followed [Jesus], *glorifying God*. And all the people, when they saw it, *gave praise to God*" (Luke 18:43; see also 7:16; 13:13; 17:15).

The Gospel writers make *the effect* of Jesus' ministry clear: the glory and praise of God.

His Own Intent

But what about Jesus' intent? What does Christ himself say about his goal in all he did?

The words of Jesus in the Gospel of John make this particularly plain. Christ says he comes *not in his own name but his Father's* (John 5:43). He welcomes the Palm Sunday praises of Psalm 118: "Blessed is he who comes *in the name of the Lord*" (John 12:13). He says, in sum, about his life,

"I honor my Father" (8:49); all that he does is *in his Father's name* (10:25).

Fittingly, then, when teaching his disciples to pray, his first utterance expresses his primary mission in life: "Father, *hallowed be your name*" (Luke 11:2; Matthew 6:9).

The Intent of His Death

When he came to his final days, in those precious last moments before his crucifixion, his purpose in life grew all the more explicit.

> *"Now is my soul troubled. And what shall I say? 'Father, save me from this hour'? But for this purpose I have come to this hour. Father, glorify your name." (John 12:27-28)*

On the night before he died, in his great high-priestly prayer, he scarcely could have been clearer about what had driven him in life and now led him to the cross. Three times he rang the bell with piercing clarity:

> *"I glorified you on earth." (John 17:4)*

> *"I have manifested your name." (v 6)*

> *"I made known to them your name." (v 26)*

Jesus dedicated his life to glorifying his Father, through making him known to his disciples. He so lived, and so spoke, that his Father would be truly revealed and duly received.

From beginning to end, without veil or apology, Jesus sought his Father's glory. No one has ever been more consecrated to the glory of the Father than his Son. This was both the goal and effect of his life and death. So much so that even a Roman soldier who witnessed his execution got the message: "When the centurion saw what had taken place, *he praised God*" (Luke 23:47).

Our Call as His People

Jesus not only modeled this calling but also explicitly draws his people into it. Not only does he seek his Father's glory, but he calls his disciples to do the same:

> *"Let your light shine before others, so that they may see your good works and give glory to your Father who is in heaven." (Matthew 5:16)*

> *"By this my Father is glorified, that you bear much fruit and so prove to be my disciples." (John 15:8)*

Now we, his church, fulfill what God intended us for. He made us *in his image*, and we display his value to the world. We, too, learn to live dedicated to God's glory—and we do so in the name of Jesus (Colossians 3:17).

Jesus, as the ultimate human and the very "image of the invisible God" (Colossians 1:15), modeled for us what we were created to be and do: to display God's glory and make him known. We now find our highest human calling: to image and reflect God's glory by becoming increasingly conformed to the God-man's image (Romans 8:29). Which means that the original destiny of humanity is realized in the gospel and in our growing likeness to Jesus. The more we are conformed to Christ, and faithfully display and testify to him, the more we fulfill that great purpose for which we were made.

Father in heaven, we marvel at the life of your Son. We stand in awe that God himself, in the person of Christ, came down and dwelled among us, as fully human, and lived a life utterly devoted to your name and renown—the life we were all designed for. Flawed and frail as we are, we want to be more like that. Conform us to your Son's image, and fulfill in us the destiny for which you made us. Teach us, through your Spirit and the examples of your people, to walk more and more in the steps of Jesus, for your honor and praise. In Jesus' name we pray. Amen.

Scripture reading: John 12:20-28

3. HE WORKED

Jesus' Unfrenzied Industry

"My Father is working until now,
and I am working."
–John 5:17

One human life in all the Scriptures towers above the others. All who came before anticipated him, and all who follow after orient to him. Nothing compares to God himself dwelling among us in a fully human soul and body. And no one accomplished the work that he accomplished.

Careful readers of the Gospels will beware of gathering up details about Jesus' life and unhitching them from where his whole life was going. Still, we do have more to learn from the life of Christ than from the events of his final week only. One theme, especially pronounced in the Gospel of John, is what we might see as the "work ethic" of Christ.

Jesus Worked

Observe, first, that Jesus did *work*—and consider what he meant by *work* rather than what we might assume. The night before he died, he prayed to his Father, as his men listened, "I glorified you on earth, having *accomplished the work that you gave me to do*" (John 17:4). In a sense, his whole life had been a single work—a "life's work," we might say. He had a calling and a commission. His Father gave him work to do. And this was *good*—a blessing, not a curse.

Jesus did not begrudge this work. Instead, he experienced a deep satisfaction in doing the work his Father had assigned him. In fact, his soul *fed* on accomplishing his Father's work, as he testified when standing by the well in Samaria. "My food is to *do the will* of him who sent me and to *accomplish his work*" (John 4:34).

Jesus also speaks in John 9 about *stewarding time* in such a life. Here he echoes Moses' prayer to "teach us to number our days" (Psalm 90:12) and Paul's exhortation to "[make] the best use of the time" (Ephesians 5:15-16). "Night is coming, when no one can work," he says; knowing this, "we must work the works of him who sent me while it is day" (John 9:4). He had an appointed season of earthly life. Eternity would come, but for now, he was on the clock. He had work to accomplish. "As long as I am in the world, I am the light of the world" (John 9:5). He even "worked" on the Sabbath, or at least he was accused of it. And he answered the charge not by saying that he wasn't working, but that "my Father is working until now, and I am working" (John 5:17).

He Did Not Only Work

The Gospels not only show us a man who worked but also one who didn't *only* work. As we have seen, his life was more than his work. He slept and rested and retreated, and called his weary disciples away to rest with him. When they had returned from their mission and "told him all that they had done and taught"—and teaching, done well, can be really hard work—he said to them:

> "'Come away by yourselves to a desolate place and rest a while.' For many were coming and going, and they had no leisure even to eat. And they went away in the boat to a desolate place by themselves."
>
> (Mark 6:30-32)

What His Work Accomplished

That Jesus worked (and didn't *only* work) is plain enough, but what did his work mean?

Much of what we have from the Gospels about his work is from his own mouth. First, he was conscious that his work—his bodily movement, exertions, and actions in the world—bore witness to his Father. Indeed, his life's work, as we saw in chapter 2, was to glorify his Father: to make him known truly and admired duly (John 17:4, 6, 26).

And Jesus' works demonstrated that the Father had sent him. "The works that the Father has given me to accomplish, the very works that I am doing, bear witness about me that the Father has sent me" (John 5:36; also 10:25, 32). Not that he was *sent* as a mere man. The way he taught (with authority: Matthew 7:29; Mark 1:22, 27; Luke 4:32; John 7:17) and the miracles he performed pointed to his being more than a prophet—to the almost unspeakable truth that this manifestly human person was somehow God himself.

> *"Even though you do not believe me, believe the*
> *works, that you may know and understand that the*
> *Father is in me and I am in the Father."*
> *(John 10:38; see also 14:10-11)*

His works, performed in the world with human words and hands, showed who he was and whose he was—just as those who rejected him showed through their works who their own "father" was (John 8:38-41).

Industry without Frenzy

Every indication we have of Jesus' life and ministry is that he was a worker, not an idler. He began by laboring in obscurity as a craftsman for thirty years. The tenor of his ministry was one of energy and industry, not laziness or lethargy.

His life was not without weariness (John 4:6); nor was it without physical rest and spiritual retreat (Mark 6:31). He did not think of his work as *his own* but as *his Father's*. And for the sake of the faith of the people his Father had given him, he expended the energy God gave him, day in and day out, to carry out his calling.

We get the clear impression from the Gospels that he was busy. He was in increasing demand. His days were long. Yet we never get the sense that he was anxious or frenzied—even when a desperate father tried to whisk him away to save a dying daughter (Mark 5:22-36). His life was busy, but he was not hurried.

He knew his calling and gave himself to it. Not without sleep or rest, but he plainly did not live for leisure. Jesus worked.

—

Father in heaven, how sobering it is that Jesus, who labored from faith, calls us "laborers" too; we are to expend energy and effort, in his name, for the good of others. Father, we acknowledge the limits of our labors. Your word is effective in a way that our work is not. And for our acceptance with you, we do not work but trust in Christ's work (Romans 4:5). Yet in him, and by the power of his Spirit, we work. Make our lives, in their own small ways, echo the imitable work ethic of your Son, even as we stand in awe of his inimitable finished work for us. In his powerful name we pray. Amen.

Scripture reading: John 9:1-7

4. HE SLEPT

The God-Man at Rest

*"He was in the stern,
asleep on the cushion."*
–Mark 4:38

The Word became flesh and slept among us. God himself in full humanity—body, heart, mind, and will—closed his eyes and went to sleep. And not once or twice, but every day.

Of his thirty-plus years dwelling here bodily, God spent roughly one-third asleep. He ate, drank, cried, and celebrated, like every other human; he also became tired—"wearied as he was from his journey" (John 4:6)—just as we become tired and weary. And this was no sin, fault, or failing in the God-man. It was human.

Yet it's one thing to sleep, and quite another to sleep through a great storm. Matthew, Mark, and Luke all tell the story of Jesus asleep in the boat. "A great windstorm arose, and the waves were breaking into the boat, so that the boat was already filling. But he was in the stern, asleep on the cushion" (Mark 4:37-38). *Waves breaking into the boat.* Not only is this a testimony to how *tired* he must have been, but also how *trusting.* What serenity of soul, what rest in his Father, that he slept in the storm.

Trusting God, Not Self
God made us to spend a third of our lives like this.

Unconscious. Inactive. Exposed. Dependent. It's a nightly reminder of our frailty and limitations. We are creatures, not the Creator. Sleep is telling us something profound. And it does so every night.

Sleep is an exercise of faith. When we lie down, close our eyes, and give ourselves over to sleep, we make ourselves vulnerable—like Saul before David, and Samson before Delilah. Jesus not only trusted his disciples—falling asleep in their presence—but he also entrusted himself to his faithful Father, to care for him and meet every essential need. "In peace I will both lie down and sleep," said God's anointed, "for you alone, O LORD, make me dwell in safety" (Psalm 4:8). What does it say for the peace in Jesus' soul that he could sleep even in the storm?

A Divine Gift

Psalm 127:2 is perhaps the Bible's signature statement on sleep:

> "It is in vain that you rise up early and go late to
> rest, eating the bread of anxious toil; for he gives to
> his beloved sleep."

God gives sleep as an expression of his love. As much as it may seem like a horrible inconvenience and a waste of time to those toiling under the sway of a productivity idol—eight hours lost every day!—sleep is a divine gift.

Life has its ups and downs, no doubt. For everything there is a season—a day to rise early, a day to go to bed late—but God did not design us to burn the candle at both ends. He doesn't mean for us to always be "on," to always feel productive. He does mean for us to recognize the glorious constraints of creatureliness, embrace the limits of our humanity, and own the humility of coming to the end of ourselves every day—

lying down, closing our eyes, and leaving not just the whole world, but also our own worlds, to him.

Bedtime rehearses the fact that *he is God and I am not*. Every night is an opportunity to "be still, and know that I am God" (Psalm 46:10).

Awake All Night

But the sanctity of sleep is not the only lesson we glean from Jesus. Don't go away yet and miss what makes it Christian. Sleep is not only a divine gift to be received and appreciated, but also a good to be sacrificed, when necessary, in the cause of love. Jesus embraced the limits of his humanity and slept, but he was also willing to deny himself sleep to gain something greater.

We have two clear instances of Jesus denying himself this natural desire and forgoing sleep when something more pressing was at hand. The first came in choosing his apostles:

> *"He went out to the mountain to pray, and all night he continued in prayer to God. And when day came, he called his disciples and chose from them twelve, whom he named apostles." (Luke 6:12-13)*

A significant decision lay before him: Which twelve men would "be with him" (Mark 3:14) and go out to represent him? Which "uneducated, common men" would one day astonish the rulers as "they recognized that they had been with Jesus" (Acts 4:13)? Whose words would his church still be reading centuries later? Faith in his Father led Jesus, in this instance, not to sleep but to all-night prayer.

The second instance came as his defining hour approached, late at night in the Garden of Gethsemane. Doubtless Jesus and his men were exhausted. As much as he encouraged them to stay awake and prepare themselves in prayer, and as much as their spirits may have been willing, their flesh was weak (Matthew 26:41). But Jesus himself, knowing what lay before him, did not give himself to sleep, but steadied and readied his soul in prayer.

"My Father, if this cannot pass unless I drink it, your will be done" (v 42).

Jesus Sacrificed His Sleep

This echoes today in the lives of those who benefit from his person and work. Jesus not only *sanctified* our sleep; he also *sacrificed* his sleep. When the time came, he was willing to deny himself God's good gift in pursuit of something greater. Sleep wasn't his god. He did not bow his knee to sleep but to his Father—which meant having a normal pattern of sleeping and also denying himself sleep, when necessary, in dependence on God and in the service of love. Both were acts of faith.

So also today, most evenings, he says to us, by his Spirit, "Come away ... and rest a while" (Mark 6:31). But that is not all he says. At times and in seasons, he comes by his Spirit and says, in the service of love, "Sleep and take your rest later on" (Matthew 26:45). There are times to receive God's gift and enjoy our sleep, and times to deny ourselves our natural desire in view of something more important.

—

Father, make us live, and sleep, like your Son: to rest in Christ, relinquish control, close our eyes, and go to bed. And to rise and forgo this good gift whenever you call us to meet others' needs in love. Father, we praise you that you are sovereign and we are not. You don't need us to run the universe. In Jesus' name we rest in your care. Amen.

Scripture reading: Mark 4:35-41

5. HE WEPT

The Human Emotions of Christ

"He was deeply moved in his spirit
and greatly troubled."
–John 11:33

He appeared to be composed as he approached the town of Bethany. The sister of his dead friend met him outside. He consoled her with truth and grace. But then he saw the other sister, manifestly more emotional. And then came his tears.

Jesus wept.

Just two simple words, and yet they carry a world of significance. John 11:35, "Jesus wept," is the shortest verse in the Bible, but one of its most powerful and insightful. Rightly was this tiniest of sentences assigned its own number. Here we find a remarkable glimpse into the glory of the Lord of the universe.

His Human Emotions

"A man of sorrows," the prophet foretold, "and acquainted with grief" (Isaiah 53:3). Yes, he was a man of sorrows, but not of his own making. "Surely he has borne *our griefs* and carried *our sorrows*" (v 4). Because his love is great, he made our pains his own.

It is not inherently impressive to have a king that cries. But it is a great comfort to have a sovereign who not only knows our frame (Psalm 103:14) and what is in us (John 2:25) but also shares in our flesh and blood (Hebrews 2:14) and is moved by compassion for his people.

God himself took our full humanity. And with it, our feelings. And with them, even our sorrows. We are finite and frail, but God gave us mighty emotions. We celebrate. We grieve. We rejoice. We weep. And we do so with Jesus as one of us.

"Christ has put on our feelings along with our flesh," wrote John Calvin. Throughout the Gospels, Jesus clearly manifests human emotions. When he heard the centurion's words of faith, "he marveled" (Matthew 8:10). He said in Gethsemane that his soul was "very sorrowful, even to death" (Matthew 26:38). Hebrews 5:7 says he prayed "with loud cries and tears."

But no one shows us the truly human emotions of Christ like his beloved disciple John, who wrote the fourth Gospel.

From Love to Tears
That Jesus loved dead Lazarus and his two sisters could not be any clearer in John 11. Verse 5: "Now Jesus *loved* Martha and her sister and Lazarus." Verse 36: the people say, in response to Jesus' weeping, "See how he *loved* him!"

Jesus wept not because he lacked faith but because he loved. In compassion, he wept with his beloved friend who wept. "When Jesus saw her weeping, and the Jews who had come with her also weeping, he was *deeply moved in his spirit and greatly troubled*" (John 11:33).

And this even when he knew that Lazarus would rise. He had already said to his followers, "This illness does not lead to death. It is for the glory of God, so that the Son of God may be glorified through it" (v 4). And again, "Our friend Lazarus has fallen asleep, but I go to awaken him" (v 11). And yet, Jesus wept.

From Anger to Tears

His tears did not flow only from his love. He had righteous anger at the realities of death and unbelief. John says he was "deeply moved in his spirit and greatly troubled"—literally, he was outraged and unsettled. He was indignant and disturbed.

The same word that is translated "deeply moved" here comes across as a stern warning elsewhere (Matthew 9:30; Mark 1:43)—even a scolding (Mark 14:5). It's a serious term. In other Greek texts, as D.A. Carson writes, "it can refer to the snorting of horses; as applied to human beings, it invariably suggests anger, outrage or emotional indignation" (*The Gospel According to John*, p 415). And Jesus was thus "deeply moved again" when he came to Lazarus's tomb in John 11:38.

But he was also "greatly troubled." He was shaken up, unsettled. As he stood face to face with death, he knew what it would take to conquer this foe. He was about to take back Lazarus from its jaws. Next time, he would lay down his own life as the ransom.

Here Comes Trouble

He would be troubled again. As his own hour came, he prayed, "Now is my soul *troubled*. And what shall I say? 'Father, save me from this hour'?" (John 12:27). As he recognized the traitor, "Jesus was *troubled in his spirit*, and testified, 'Truly, truly, I say to you, one of you will betray me'" (13:21).

This was a trouble that was his own to face. His disciples could not do this with him. Indeed, he did it for them. And so he said, "Let not your hearts be troubled" (14:1), and again, "Let not your hearts be troubled, neither let them be afraid" (v 27). He would face this fear, striding into the very furnace, so that they would be spared it.

But in John 11, the love of verses 5 and 36 and the outrage of verse 33 led to the tears of verse 35. Because he loved, and because he was staring death in the face—because he was outraged at its evil and determined that it must not endure—Jesus wept.

Such tears stem from no lack of faith. This weeping is precisely the response of faith. "The same sin and death," says Carson, "the same unbelief, that prompted his outrage, also generated his grief. Those who follow Jesus as his disciples today do well to learn the same tension—that grief and compassion without outrage will diminish to mere sentiment, while outrage without grief will harden into self-righteous arrogance and irascibility" (p 416).

From Tears to Action

Jesus' weeping did not come from despair and resignation. These were not the tears of one who had realized he was powerless and was ready to give up. Rather, these were the tears of mingled affection and anger, leading to action. He would raise Lazarus—and give his own life.

Lazarus's death was overcome, but that didn't mean it was not to be mourned. And Jesus' own death would be the great overcoming, but it would not be without its excruciating pain. He would walk through the greatest of sorrows. He would cry, "My God, my God, why have you forsaken me?" (Matthew 27:46).

When Lazarus had been raised, Jesus would return to the Calvary road for his final showdown with sin and death.

—

O Father in heaven, what grace we see in the tears of your Son. He wept. In him we see that you do not stand aloof from the pains of our existence. You have drawn near. You have taken our flesh and blood in Christ. You have not called us to a humanity that your Son was unwilling to take. We suffer no pain he was unwilling to bear, no grief he was unwilling to carry.

And so we look forward to that day when you will wipe away every tear—not because you will suppress our sadness but because Christ has shed his own tears and has triumphed. In his precious name we pray. Amen.

Scripture reading: John 11:28-37

6. HE WALKED

The Pace of Christian Love

Jesus went on from there and
walked beside the Sea of Galilee.
—Matthew 15:29

Will you excuse me for wondering if the apostle Paul was a runner? Running is a curiously common theme in his sermons and letters. He referred to his own life and ministry as running (1 Corinthians 9:26; Galatians 2:2; Philippians 2:16) and described the Galatians' (past) faith in similar terms: "You were running well" (Galatians 5:7). He also asked the Thessalonians to pray for him, "that the word of the Lord may speed [run] ahead and be honored" (2 Thessalonians 3:1). He preached in Antioch about John the Baptist "finishing his course" (Acts 13:25), expressed to the Ephesian elders his desire that "I may finish my course" (Acts 20:24), and wrote in his final letter, "I have finished the race" (2 Timothy 4:7).

While *walking* serves as his more common image of the Christian life (nearly thirty times in his letters), Paul had a place for speaking in more intense, even aggressive terms as well—of a kind of athletic capacity in the Christian life, as he wrote so memorably to the Corinthians:

"Do you not know that in a race all the runners run,
but only one receives the prize? So run that you may
obtain it." (1 Corinthians 9:24)

Moving at the Pace of Love

Jesus, too, as we celebrated in chapter 3, was no stranger to effort and exertion. He had a sterling work ethic, and yet we never get the impression that he was in a hurry. He worked—and he walked.

The life of Christ was not idle, nor was it frenzied. He walked. And he walked. And he walked. From all we can tell from the Gospels, Jesus' days were full. He was busy, yet he did not seem to be rushing. One way we might say it is that Jesus *moved at the pace of love* (not that Paul didn't). And don't we all want to be like that?

"My Little Daughter"

Of the many instances in the Gospels where Jesus is on his feet, moving from town to town and region to region, one stands out in my mind as a glimpse of the pace of love—a pace that neither stalls in idleness nor rushes ahead leaving hurting people in its wake.

It begins with him, again, on the move—first to "the other side of the sea, to the country of the Gerasenes" (Mark 5:1), and then back again to Galilee (v 21), where a synagogue official named Jairus approaches (v 22-24). This man falls to his knees to plead for help: "My little daughter is at the point of death. Come and lay your hands on her, so that she may be made well and live" (v 23). Jairus doesn't just say "daughter," but "my little daughter." It is a term of endearment and particular care—a glimpse into this father's heart.

Time to Wake Up

Jesus picks up on Jairus's term of endearment, and later when he arrives at the house—after she has already died—and takes her by the hand, he says, "*Little girl*, I say to you, arise" (v 41). Not just "girl," but "little girl"—an expression of compassion and holy condescension, like the term her father used when he called her "my little daughter." We learn she's twelve years old, which isn't "little" today, and wasn't in the first century, when some 12-year-olds were on the brink of marriage. "My little daughter" and "little girl" are not statements of fact as much as expressions of a tender, affectionate, and protective fatherly heart.

The account ends, of course, with Jesus raising this young girl from the dead. It is a stunning sneak glimpse into who he is—not only a great teacher but God himself. Mark piles on language to describe how astounded are the girl's parents and the three disciples. Literally, "they were astonished with great amazement" (v 42). They knew he could heal, but reclaim someone from death? This is an astounding display of his power and his identity.

By raising Jairus's daughter, Jesus shows ahead of time that his Father has power over the final enemy. He treats death as if it were only sleep: "Sweetie, it's time to wake up."

Another Daughter

But Mark 5:21-43 isn't just about the little girl. There's also an older woman—another daughter. This is where Jesus' walking, his pace of love, shines.

On the way to heal Jairus's daughter, with the crowd pressing in on Jesus, a woman with a chronic disease reached out and touched his garment from behind. Jesus felt that "power had gone out from him" (v 30), and the woman "felt in her body that she was healed of her disease" (v 29). Jesus stopped and turned around to ask who had touched him. Bewildered and impatient, his disciples asked, "You see the crowd pressing around you, and yet you say, 'Who touched me?'" (v 31). Besides, Jairus's daughter was on her deathbed! *Jesus, if ever there were a time to run, it's now. There is no time for this woman when a 12-year-old girl is about to die!* But Jesus had the time.

Go in Peace

The woman steps forward, and, far from rebuking her, Jesus shows her a father's heart for a daughter. "Daughter, your faith has made you well; go in peace, and be healed of your disease" (v 34). He wants her to know that it's not her superstitious reach that has healed her but her faith. And he calls her *daughter*. Just as Jairus has shown the unique tenderness and compassion of a father's heart for his little daughter, now Jesus shows us his heart—God's heart—for one of his daughters. And he does so when he is under pressure from Jairus and his own disciples to hurry on to something far more urgent.

Of course, we are not Jesus. We cannot raise a daughter who has already died, nor are we expected to. But oh, how we want to learn from the life of God himself among us—who in the midst of life's pressures trusted his Father. He was not distracted by the past or hurrying into the future. Fully present in the moment, Jesus walked.

—

Father, in a day of acceleration, would you slow our souls and steps to the pace of love? Remind us again and again why you put us here, and why, for now, you keep us here. It is not for us to make a name for ourselves or secure our heaven with our work, nor to pretend we have our heaven now. Like Jesus, we want to walk in faith. One foot in front of the other. Day after day. To walk with you, to find the pace to which you've called us, and to see and meet the needs of others. Help us to walk like Jesus. In his name we pray. Amen.

Scripture reading: Mark 5:21-43

7. HE TAUGHT

Marveling at the Words of Christ

"All the people were hanging on his words."
—Luke 19:48

"**N**o one ever spoke like this man!" Even his enemies had to admit it.

Jerusalem was teeming with travelers during the Feast of Booths, and Jesus was teaching in the temple. A new excitement was in the air. And controversy. Some said he was a good man; others thought he was leading people astray (John 7:12).

The Pharisees overheard the muttering and conspired with their political rivals, the chief priests, to send officers, ready to arrest Jesus if he misspoke.

Some wondered if this was the Prophet who was to come. Or even the Christ himself. Others argued that David's heir would not come from Galilee. The officers, equally stunned, returned with empty hands—and open mouths—to the chief priests and Pharisees, who asked, "Why did you not bring him?" (v 45).

John then reports, as he loves to do, a word on the lips of Jesus' enemies that is even truer than they know: "No one ever spoke like this man!" (v 46).

All Things Well

The words and teaching of Jesus are unmatched. But a tension runs through his ministry from start to finish. Time and again, his fame spread because of his miracles. Word spread like wildfire because of his works. People wanted to see what the Gospel of John calls "signs." Yet Jesus never self-identified as a miracle-worker. He was a teacher—whose words amazed his hearers as much as his healings, and more.

Nicodemus captures it well, even though he still has much to learn, when he comes to Jesus at night in John 3: "Rabbi, we know that you are a teacher come from God, for no one can do these signs that you do unless God is with him" (v 2). The signs point. The *works* that dazzle the eyes are meant to open ears to the *words* of a teacher who has come from God.

Himself the Word of God, Jesus spoke words that were like the words of no other before him, in his day, or since. He opened his mouth to teach, and soon "all the people were hanging on his words" (Luke 19:48).

Amazed and Astonished

Even at the age of twelve, two decades before he went public as a teacher, his words amazed and astonished people as he sat among the teachers in the temple: "All who heard him were *amazed* at his understanding and his answers. And when his parents saw him, they were *astonished*" (Luke 2:47-48).

When Jesus spoke, his words, not just his works, were arresting. He "amazed" the crowds with miracles (Mark 1:27; 2:12; 5:42), but he also "amazed" his disciples with his teaching (10:24, 32). As the masses were "astonished" at his works (Mark 7:37; Luke 5:9; 9:43; 11:38), so, even more, those with ears to hear were "astonished" at his words (Mark 1:22; 6:2; 10:26; 11:18).

Significantly, Matthew reports that at the end of the famous Sermon on the Mount, "when Jesus finished these sayings, the crowds were astonished at his teaching, for he was teaching them as one who had authority, and not as their scribes" (Matthew 7:28-29). And when he taught in his hometown, Nazareth, "they were astonished, and said, 'Where did this man get this wisdom and these mighty works?'" (13:54).

When he moved on to the next town, Capernaum, the people there, too, "were astonished at his teaching, for his word possessed authority" (Luke 4:32). And when it seemed to matter most, during his Passion week, with the chief priests trying to trip him up, he not only answered flawlessly but went on the offensive. "And when the crowd heard it, they were astonished at his teaching" (Matthew 22:33).

They Marveled

Even more than being "amazed" and "astonished," the Gospels report that Jesus' hearers often *marveled*. They "marveled at the gracious words that were coming from his mouth" (Luke 4:22).

When the Pharisees "plotted how to entangle him in his words" (Matthew 22:15), Luke reports the upshot: "They were not able ... to catch him in what he said, but *marveling* at his answer they became silent" (Luke 20:26). He could open his mouth and make them put their hands over their own. Which brings us back to John 7 and the clearest explanation of what made his teaching so marvelous.

What Was It about His Words?

As Jesus taught during the feast, the establishment "marveled" and asked, "How is it that this man has learning, when he has never studied?" (John 7:15).

Jesus answers with the most focused and penetrating words he has to say about his words. Here he pulls back the curtain, as it were, and *teaches about his teaching*. In doing so, he gives us a profound insight into what sets his words and teaching apart:

"My teaching is not mine, but his who sent me." (v 16)

Beneath the enigma of "his teaching" not being "his" is this bracing clarity: Who gets the glory? Whose honor is it for?

> *"If anyone's will is to do God's will, he will know whether the teaching is from God or whether I am speaking on my own authority. The one who speaks on his own authority seeks his own glory; but the one who seeks the glory of him who sent him is true, and in him there is no falsehood." (v 17-18)*

Who gets the glory? For most teachers, the answer is painfully plain: we seek our own. Apart from Christ, we teach for our own benefit, advancement, and praise. Yet the God-man himself—fully God, yes, and among us as fully man—*seeks not his own glory* in his teaching but pursues the glory of the one who sent him.

Yes, "no one ever spoke like *this man*"—because no man ever lived for the name and glory of God like the one named Jesus (John 17:4, 6, 26). What that dedication of mind and heart brought to his words made a difference everywhere he went and every time he taught.

—

Father in heaven, may we never treat "for your glory" as a throwaway phrase. We want to live for your glory, like your Son, and use our words for your honor and praise, like he did. Father, thank you for your word to us in Jesus, and his astounding, marvelous words to us and our world. Saturate our lives in your words. Change our lives with them. Empower our love with them. And make us, too, like Jesus, to make much of you with our teaching and the words we speak. In his name we pray. Amen.

Scripture reading: Matthew 22:15-22

8. HE DISCIPLED

Blessing the Masses, Investing in a Few

"He appointed twelve (whom he also named apostles)
so that they might be with him."
—Mark 3:14

Perhaps one of the biggest surprises in a careful reading of the Gospels is how Jesus' ministry revolved around his investment in his twelve men.

Jesus did indeed *bless the masses* with his public teaching, but he gave the lion's share of his time to *investing in the few*: his followers, and especially the twelve men whom we call his "apostles" or "disciples." After more than three decades of life in the obscurity of a backwater town called Nazareth, his entry into public ministry came not by gathering a crowd but by pursuing a small group of disciples and calling them to a particular season of learning under him. "Follow me, and I will make you fishers of men" (Matthew 4:19).

For three and a half years, they learned under his personal tutelage and care. And having been discipled by him, there would have been little doubt in their minds about what their Master was calling them to when he said, after his resurrection, before his departure, "Make disciples of all nations" (Matthew 28:19).

So also we see the echo of Jesus' disciple-making in the ministry of the apostle Paul, who had been discipled by a rabbi in his youth. Though Paul himself did not study under Jesus like Peter, James, and John, he did follow suit, as one untimely born (1 Corinthians 15:8) in his personal investments in younger associates. Timothy and Titus are well known among them; there were many others. And Paul charged Timothy to keep the pattern: to disciple the church's next generation of leaders, and to teach them to do the same (2 Timothy 2:2).

What Is Disciple-Making?

Disciple-making, as I'm using the term, is the process in which a maturing believer invests him or herself, for a particular period of time, in one or just a few younger believers, in order to help them grow in the faith—including helping them to invest in others who will invest in others.

It's especially vital for new and young believers. A discipler is like a personal trainer to help get you going. The goal for the disciple isn't to always have the personal trainer watching over you, but to learn spiritual health and fitness for yourself, under God, and then to be able to train others.

Such disciple-making requires both structure and some margin that allows the discipler to speak spontaneously into teachable moments. It's both engineered and organic, trellis and vine, truth-speaking and life-sharing. Quantity time is the soil in which quality time grows.

The vast majority of Jesus' time with his men wasn't formal. Mark 3:14 says, "He appointed twelve (whom he also named apostles) so that they might *be with him*." Before he sent them out to preach on his behalf, they first needed to be with their Master. Not with a clock ticking in the background but with the space and time and overlap of everyday life that encourages the kind of effect that Jesus had on his men.

It is nothing short of amazing, what three years with Christ did for this ragtag band of young Galileans—fishermen and a tax collector among them. All of them were outsiders to the religious establishment of the time; none of them were rabbi-trained like Paul. And yet, after Christ's ascension and the pouring out of his Spirit, the religious authorities could see with their own eyes the profound imprints of Christ on his men:

> *"Now when they saw the boldness of Peter and John, and perceived that they were uneducated, common men, they were astonished. And they recognized that they had been with Jesus." (Acts 4:13)*

Till Harvest Comes

Jesus' parable of the man scattering seed, while not narrowly about disciple-making, captures the dynamic of how God works life-change through the daily modest investments of disciplers.

> *"The kingdom of God is as if a man should scatter seed on the ground. He sleeps and rises night and day, and the seed sprouts and grows; he knows not how. The earth produces by itself, first the blade, then the ear, then the full grain in the ear. But when the grain is ripe, at once he puts in the sickle, because the harvest has come." (Mark 4:26-29)*

Disciple-making is often like that. The discipler scatters his seed. He sleeps and rises night and day. The seed sprouts and grows almost imperceptibly—"he knows not how." There are not clear cause-and-effect relationships between the various investments a discipler makes and the maturation and growth in those in whom he or she invests. But the discipler keeps investing. And God gives the growth. The blade, the ear, then the full grain in the ear. And all of a sudden, the harvest comes. We see a changed life and say, "God did it! God did it again."

As with farming, we typically don't see the organic progress in the day-to-day but over the course of months—and then it's amazing what a harvest can happen. All of a sudden, in a moment, God takes off the blinders, and we realize what kind of growth has been happening right before our eyes, hidden in plain view. It shows that the glory belongs to him, not to us.

We pivot now from the life of Christ—his purpose, his habits, his rest, his sorrows, his work, his pace, and his teaching—to the meaning and achievements of his sacrificial death. His massive investments in his Twelve (with, tragically, one to be lost) take on even more significance in light of what's to come. Jesus would not always be with them. In fact, his time among them would be only little more than three years. He would do his unique work at the cross and finish his course, and leave behind only a band of painfully ordinary Galileans. But Jesus did not cut corners on the preparation of his men. They were his first work, until it came time to do his cross-work. Then, they were ready. He would send his Spirit. He would change the world through them.

—

Father, give us the wherewithal, like Jesus, to invest in the lives of others in ways that cannot be replaced by mass production. Make us faithful in the seemingly small things which, in your economy, turn out to be big. In a world of distraction and hurry and overcommitment, give us the grace to go deep in the lives of a few. In our heart to bless many, may we not neglect to invest in one or two. Give us the foresight, patience, and steadfastness of your Son, and pour out your Spirit on us and on those in whom we invest. In Jesus' name we ask. Amen.

Scripture reading: Acts 4:5-13

Part 2

HIS DEATH

"The life I now live in the flesh
I live by faith in the Son of God,
who loved me and gave himself for me."
–Galatians 2:20

9. WHAT MAKES A CROSS WONDERFUL?

"We preach Christ crucified,
a stumbling block to Jews and folly to Gentiles,
but to those who are called, both Jews and Greeks,
Christ the power of God and the wisdom of God."
—1 Corinthians 1:23-24

How can a cross be *wonderful*? Puritan pastor and prolific hymn writer Isaac Watts (1674–1748) wrote, in the first couplet of one of the most cherished of his songs, of "the wondrous cross / On which the Prince of glory died." It is a striking phrase, "wondrous cross."

The cross—that odious Roman method of public execution? In the sordid history of human evil, few paths of execution have been more painful and shameful than that of death by crucifixion. And yet that cross is somehow *wonderful*?

Saying that the cross is wondrous would be like saying today that the electric chair is magnificent, or that lethal injection is delightful, or that death by firing squad is beautiful. Wouldn't only a sick and deranged person put labels like *wonderful* and *beautiful* on such a horrible and tragic event as the destruction of human life? With the cross being one of the most horrible of all, on the one hand, and with the tragedy compounded immeasurably by the fact that the one executed did not deserve to die?

Yes—unless something supernatural is at work. In natural terms, simply nothing was wonderful about the crucifixion of an innocent man on a hill outside Jerusalem. But God's ways are not our ways. His thoughts are not our thoughts; they are higher (Isaiah 55:8-9). And with the eyes of faith, we see the wonder, even in the cross.

He Chose to Shame the Wise

Few texts in Scripture lead us to see the wonder and the horror of the crucifixion like 1 Corinthians 1:23-24. There Paul writes:

> *"We preach Christ crucified, a stumbling block to Jews and folly to Gentiles, but to those who are called, both Jews and Greeks, Christ the power of God and the wisdom of God."*

To those without faith, the crucifixion of Jesus of Nazareth—whose followers claimed he was not only "the Christ," the long-awaited Jewish Messiah, but God himself in humanity—was not wonderful. And the preaching of it, to unbelievers, did not seem powerful or wise.

For his own people, the Jews, the crucified Christ was a stumbling block: a great obstacle to embracing him as the one on whom God's special messianic favor rested. How could God allow his Christ—indeed, his own divine Son—to be condemned and executed by the Romans? "Cursed is everyone who is hanged on a tree," read the Jewish Scriptures (Galatians 3:13; Deuteronomy 21:23). *Surely, this couldn't be the long-awaited Messiah,* many people thought. *God would never have let such a lowly and powerless end come to his Anointed One.*

For the Greeks, such a shameful and terrible execution had nothing of the ring of human wisdom, which was what they were seeking. It is counter to the natural human instinct, to believe that the God in whom we live and move and have our being would bring such a fate on his own Son. *This is sheer foolishness,* thought Greek-trained minds—at least those which did not have the help of the Holy Spirit to open their eyes to the glory.

So too for us today. The cross humbles us—our assumptions, our expectations, our default patterns and ways of life. Without the aid of the Spirit, the eyes of our hearts remain blind. We perceive merely in a natural, human way.

But Paul counters both the Jewish and Greek suspicions with the unsuspected power and wisdom of God, and the wonder of the cross:

> *"God chose what is foolish in the world to shame the wise; God chose what is weak in the world to shame the strong; God chose what is low and despised in the world, even things that are not, to bring to nothing things that are, so that no human being might boast in the presence of God."*
> *(1 Corinthians 1:27-29)*

That Terrible, Horrible, Wonderful Cross

We call that dreadful day on which Jesus died "Good Friday" because, when God's Holy Spirit has opened our eyes, we see through the horror of that day to the glory of Easter Sunday. When we see that Jesus died not for his own sins but for ours, so that we could be restored to him and his Father forever, we begin to see the wonder of the cross breaking through all the awfulness. Even as we cringe, at one level, at the unspeakable tragedy, we can say, "How marvelous!" Even at the very moment when we see sin rise to its ugliest height in the conspiracy to murder God himself, we can say, "What beauty!"

For those of us who have received the gift of the new birth, the enlightening of the eyes of our hearts, and who have begun to taste the joy of life with Jesus—which will grow and sweeten and deepen for all eternity—this is a won-derful cross. This is where the "old me" decisively died and where the "new me" came to life.

And this is where God himself, against the darkest and most gruesome of backdrops, showed climactically, for the eyes of faith, what wondrous love he has for us (Romans 5:8). Wonder upon wonder: here, at the cross, of all places, is where we see most clearly the Father's demonstration of his love for his people. And here, no less, do we see Christ's love for his bride. "Christ loved the church and gave himself up for her" (Ephesians 5:25).

So, as we move from the marvels of Christ's life to the fact and facets of his death, the mood not only becomes more serious but simultaneously more wonderful. We linger at Calvary, and over the precious blood he spilled for us. As we do so, with eyes opened and illumined by his Spirit, we see beyond the horror of his gruesome execution to the glory of what he obtained for us.

—

Father, do this miracle in us, as you've done now for two millen-nia in your people, of seeing not only horror at that hill outside Jerusalem but also wonder. Even as you shock us again with a reality almost too great to appreciate—that your own divine Son, in human flesh, died—plant fresh amazement in us that this was for us, his death for our life. Strike us with Jesus' will-ingness to die, so that we might see in it not some accident of history but the single greatest demonstration of love there could ever be. Put awe in our hearts and praise in our mouths as we admire the achievements of our dear Savior for us at the cross. In his sweet and sacrificial name we pray. Amen.

Scripture reading: 1 Corinthians 1:20-31

10. WHAT MAKES BLOOD PRECIOUS?

Five Benefits Christ Purchased

"He entered once for all into the holy places,
not by means of the blood of goats and calves
but by means of his own blood,
thus securing an eternal redemption."
—Hebrews 9:12

One way we see wonder in Jesus' cross is in singing of the power of his blood.

There is pow'r, pow'r, wonder-working pow'r
In the precious blood of the Lamb.
("Power in the Blood," Lewis E. Jones)

Christians of all stripes affirm that there is indeed *power in the blood* of Jesus. But have you ever paused to ask *how?* Is it magic blood? How do we explain this *power?*

What Does the Blood Do?

Throughout the Bible, blood represents life (for instance, Genesis 9:4), and the spilling or shedding of blood depicts death (Leviticus 17:11, 14; Deuteronomy 12:23). Because the just penalty for human sin is death (Romans 6:23), God prescribed and permitted animal sacrifices to stand in *temporarily* for the requirement of death when his people sinned.

But one day a reckoning had to come.

Christians believe and celebrate the truth that now, in Christ, that reckoning has come. Jesus willingly "offered himself" (Hebrews 9:14) by "once for all" shedding "his own blood" (v 12). What the temporary animal sacrifices had anticipated, Christ's blood did permanently and decisively.

The apostle Paul, in particular, celebrates the manifold grace that comes to us *because of Jesus' blood*. Five times Paul makes the connection explicit between Jesus' *blood* and a specific aspect of what he secured for us at the cross. We could meditate on these five for a lifetime and still not get to the bottom of them. Some of them we'll look at further in the chapters to come.

Propitiation: To Remove God's Righteous Wrath

Romans 3:25 says Jesus is the one whom "God put forward as a *propitiation by his blood*, to be received by faith." Because God is just, the sins of his people are no small obstacle. In his justice, he cannot sweep our sins—which are acts of cosmic treason against him—under the rug of the universe. There must be "propitiation," the appeasement of his righteous anger against sin. Yet, in his love, God devised a way to satisfy justice and still triumph with mercy.

God himself, in the person of his own Son, took on human flesh and blood, and offered himself in the place of sinners. The Son received the just wrath of God and paid our penalty in his death, that we might live. His blood *propitiated* God's righteous wrath, upheld divine justice, and opened to us—to all who receive this by faith—the floodgates of his mercy.

Justification: To Extend God's Full Acceptance

Romans 5:9 says, "We have now been justified by his blood." *Justified* is courtroom language. The prosecution and the defense each present their case, and the judge or jury makes a declaration. The defendant is either *guilty as charged* or declared to be in right standing with the law— *righteous. Justified.*

The reason why those who are united to Jesus by faith are *justified* is owing, in part, to his sacrificial and substitutionary death. He willingly shed his own blood, not for his own sin—he had none—but for ours. When we are joined to him by faith, our sins are covered by the spilling of his blood, so we are no longer judged *guilty*, and his perfect obedience is counted as our own, so we are now declared *righteous*. Without his blood, our unrighteousness would remain unaddressed. With it, we can stand and receive with him his Father's declaration, "Righteous."

Redemption: To Purchase Our True Freedom

Ephesians 1:7 says, "In him we have redemption through his blood, the forgiveness of our trespasses." To *redeem* means to buy back, or to secure the freedom of someone in bondage. Because of our sins, we all were (and many continue to be) in spiritual captivity. The devil had power over us because of our violations of God's law. But in Christ, by the shedding of his blood, God purchased our freedom from the penalty demanded by justice and from the power of Satan. "Having forgiven us all our trespasses, by canceling the record of debt that stood against us with its legal demands" (Colossians 2:13-14), Jesus "disarmed the rulers and authorities and put them to open shame" (v 15).

The decisive weapon the demons had against us was unforgiven sin, but when Jesus spilled his own blood in our place, he liberated us.

Reconciliation: To Restore Our Best Relationship

Ephesians 2:13 puts forgiveness at the fore: "Now in Christ Jesus you who once were far off have been brought near by the blood of Christ." At the heart of this bringing near is the reconciliation of humans with our Creator. Our sin and rebellion against God put an impassable chasm between us, but now, in Christ, the relationship is restored. Christ grants us personal access to his Father—access that we, born into sin, never could have secured.

Paul is not just speaking on an individual level here. In the past, God drew near to his covenant people, then called Israel. But now, in the new covenant, he draws near not to a particular ethnic people but to all who receive his Son in faith—no matter how far away they have run. In fact, the phrase "brought near by the blood of Christ" gestures to what each of these divine gifts in Jesus' blood does for us: *they bring us to God* (1 Peter 3:18).

Pacification: To Make Peace with God Himself

Finally, in Christ, God reconciles his people "to himself ... making peace by the blood of his cross" (Colossians 1:19-20). That Jesus shed his blood *on the cross* has been implicit in each instance, but here Paul makes it plain. It is "the blood of his cross" that makes peace between God and humans. He *made peace* by means of history's most notorious instrument of torture and execution.

Jesus did not shed his blood by accident. Tragic as his death was, it was deliberate and voluntary. He spilled his blood on purpose at the cross. At bottom, his life was not taken; he gave it. In doing so, he absorbed the righteous wrath of God against our sin, granted us his full legal acceptance, purchased our true freedom, restored our most important relationship, and made peace for us with God himself. This is how, as Paul says elsewhere, he secured "the church of God, which he obtained with his own blood" (Acts 20:28).

Precious Blood

What an ocean of grace is in that last line of the familiar chorus: "In the precious blood of the Lamb." Precious indeed. That pairing of *precious* with Jesus' blood comes from the apostle Peter, who writes about "*the precious blood of Christ, like that of a lamb without blemish or spot*" (1 Peter 1:19).

It is fitting to sing of his "wondrous cross" and "precious blood" and the glory he secured for us then and there, of all times and places, in his death.

—

Father in heaven, how precious is the blood of Christ! What a wonder that you sent him. What a wonder that he came. And how precious is all that his death accomplished. The blood he shed, the life he gave, the death he embraced—it was all for us. So, Father, we thank you for the blood of Jesus. That he became one of us and took on human flesh and blood. And that he lovingly, willingly spilled his blood, to the point of death, for us. In his precious name we pray. Amen.

Scripture reading: Romans 5:6-11

11. BARABBAS AND ME

A Substitute for the Guilty

*"He released the man who had been thrown into prison
for insurrection and murder, for whom they asked,
but he delivered Jesus over to their will."*
–Luke 23:25

Barabbas. He was a scoundrel, and worse. A "notorious prisoner" (Matthew 27:16); a rebel and murderer (Mark 15:7). Luke introduces him as "a man who had been thrown into prison for an insurrection started in the city and for murder" (Luke 23:19). Manifestly guilty, he deserved to die, in both Roman and Jewish eyes. This was no minor offender in rehab, but a murderer on death row.

Along with the plotting Jewish leaders, spineless Pilate, contemptuous Herod, and treacherous Judas, Barabbas is one of the certifiable bad guys of the Passion narratives—and he goes free. While Jesus, our innocent hero, is falsely accused, outrageously reviled, flogged, *and crucified*.

Jesus the Innocent

A particular emphasis of Luke's carefully crafted telling of the day of Jesus' death is that he was innocent and *did not deserve to die*. Luke strikes the notes not just once or twice but again and again in Luke 23. First, in verse 4, Pilate declares, "I find no guilt in this man." Then, in verses 14-15, Pilate notes that not only had he previously declared Jesus innocent, but Herod had too: "Behold, I did not find this man guilty of any of your charges against him. Neither did Herod, for he sent him back to us."

Pilate then declares Jesus' innocence three more times in the span of only eight verses (v 15-22). Verse 15: "Look, nothing deserving death has been done by him." Verse 20: "Pilate addressed them once more, desiring to release Jesus." Verse 22: "A third time [Pilate] said to them, 'Why, what evil has he done? I have found in him no guilt deserving death.'"

Then, later in Luke 23, Jesus' innocence is echoed yet again, both by the thief on the cross and by the centurion. In verse 41, one thief says to the other, "We are receiving the due reward of our deeds; but this man has done nothing wrong." Then, finally, at Jesus' death, the centurion declares, unbidden, in verse 47, "Certainly this man was innocent!"

Why would Luke make so much of Jesus' innocence? Why so carefully tell us that Pilate initially found no guilt in Jesus, then that neither did Herod, then that Pilate declared Jesus' innocence three more times, and finally that not only the thief on the cross but also the centurion recognized this innocence?

Barabbas the Guilty

It is just after Pilate begins to plead for some sanity—"Look, nothing deserving death has been done by him"—that Luke introduces Barabbas: "But they all cried out together, 'Away with this man, and release to us Barabbas'" (v 18). *Release the scoundrel manifestly guilty of murder and rebellion.* Rebellion was precisely what the leaders and prevailing voices in the crowd had charged Jesus with when they said he was "misleading the people" (v 14) and "saying that he himself is Christ, a king" (v 2).

Upon Barabbas's release, Luke reiterates his guilt: "[Pilate] released the man who had been thrown into prison *for insurrection and murder*" (v 25). In other words, remember Barabbas's guilt, as charged. He is the one, not Jesus, who *deserves death*.

The First Substitute

Jesus is innocent. Barabbas is guilty. Yet here Luke means for us to identify not only with Jesus, our hero, but also, surprisingly, with Barabbas. He embodies our plight as rebels deserving death, in need of saving.

Jesus, the innocent, is delivered over to the punishment of death; while the guilty one, deserving of death, is released and given new life. This was a foretaste of the grace that will be unleashed at the cross. Just as Jesus' death sentence leads to the release of the physical captive Barabbas, so also his condemnation leads to the release of a multitude of spiritual captives from every tribe, tongue, people, and nation.

As Pilate releases Barabbas, the guilty, and delivers over to death Jesus, the innocent, we have a picture of our own release effected by the cross through faith. In Barabbas, we have a glimpse of our death-deserving guilt and a preview of the astonishing grace of Jesus and his embrace of the cross, through which we are set free.

Here, as Jesus is delivered to death and Barabbas goes free, we have the first substitution of the cross. The innocent Jesus is condemned as a sinner, while the guilty sinner is released as if innocent.

I Am Barabbas

As we approach the cross of Christ today, we identify with our Savior, whose death is our death. We cling to him in faith. His condemning of sin is our condemning of sin. But we also identify, as sinners, with Barabbas. We are rebels who have broken God's law, guilty as charged, deserving death for our rebellion against our Creator and the ruler of the universe. Jesus, through the grace of giving himself for us at the cross, has taken our place—as our substitute—and we are released.

As we more greatly understand the depths of our sin, we come to see, in some sense, that *I am Barabbas*. I am the one so clearly guilty and deserving of condemnation. I am the one set free because of the willing substitution of the Son of God in my place. "Those who are well have no need of a physician, but those who are sick," Jesus says in Mark 2:17. "I came not to call the righteous, but sinners."

—

Father in heaven, we stand in awe of Jesus, our innocent substitute, who stood in our place to receive the penalty for our sin, not his. What a true and full atonement—removing the chasm between you and us because of our sin and restoring us to familial nearness and oneness through faith in Christ. We claim him. In faith, we rest our souls on Christ. He is our payment for the penalty we justly deserve. He is our substitute. Before your holiness, God, we cling to Christ as our covering and treasure— not just our saving but our Savior. In his spectacular name we pray. Amen.

Scripture reading: Luke 23:13-25

12. HE TOOK THE WRATH FOR US

The Glory of Propitiation

*"Christ redeemed us from the curse of the law
by becoming a curse for us."*
–Galatians 3:13

Great hymns, as we have seen—whether about Christ's "wondrous cross" or his "precious blood"—have the ability to unite the family of God throughout history and around the world, in the truths that matter most. But when voices from within the church begin to question or deny what the church holds most dear, great hymns also become flashpoints of controversy.

Such is the case with the modern-day song "In Christ Alone" by Keith Getty and Stuart Townend. The second verse includes these lines:

Till on that cross as Jesus died,
The wrath of God was satisfied.

Some critics find this second line uncomfortable enough to change it, skip the verse, or abandon the song altogether. The Father *satisfied his wrath* on his Son? Some allege "cosmic child abuse," or at least feel discomfort in talking in these terms, and alter the line to read "the love of God was magnified."

But as we walk this stretch of our journey, glorying in particular at the achievements of Christ for us *in his death*, it is good for us to see that the controversial line, offensive as it may be to modern palates, is deeply biblical and profoundly good news. The thought of God's righteous, omnipotent wrath against us does make us tremble—and it should. But we are not left without a refuge to run to in Christ.

Love Magnified

It's certainly true, as we have already seen, that the love of God was magnified at the cross. Romans 5:8 says, "God shows his love for us in that while we were still sinners, Christ died for us." And in Galatians 2:20, the apostle Paul refers to the magnifying of love at the cross when he speaks of Jesus as the one "who loved me" and who therefore "gave himself for me."

The cross, as the pinnacle of God's expression of his love for his people, is the most magnificent single act of love in all of history. "Greater love has no one than this, that someone lay down his life for his friends" (John 15:13)—and even greater still was it when the Son of God himself offered up his life for sinners who had rebelled against him.

Death Deserved

So, yes, "the love of God was magnified" at the cross. But why would some want to change the original lyrics, from one true line to another? Because they suspect the original to be untrue, and find it offensive to their sentiments—or the sentiments of others. Unless your mind has been shaped deeply by God's self-revelation in the Bible, rather than the prevailing winds of society today, you will find it offensive when God tells us in Scripture that we all, every one of us, are sinners. We were all born as rebels against him, and we all have lived that out, behaving as such. We all have sinned. And "the wages of sin is death" (Romans 6:23).

All human sin is high treason against the God who made us and to whom we owe ultimate allegiance. Our sin is an affront to him. And it is such a serious offense for us finite creatures to rebel against our infinite Creator that the just punishment for our sin, even in the seemingly smallest of expressions, is eternal death. God is the infinitely valuable absolute Person, and any sin against him, whether we think of it as big or small, is incalculably egregious. The just punishment for it is an eternal punishment in hell.

Unless the grace of God intervenes.

Wrath Satisfied

Where does the wrath of God come in? It is his righteous response to the outrage that sin is. Note this well: it would not be good news if God were unrighteous, if he just swept sin under the rug, if he were not angry with genocidal dictators and the pimps of child prostitution. The love of God wouldn't be comforting for long if God did not burn with righteous anger when evil people assault the weak and vulnerable. If God were to stand idly by indefinitely, without wrath, when his loved ones were abused and hurt and mistreated, then we wouldn't be very impressed or consoled by his love.

Because God is justly angry with human sin, the death of Christ at the cross was not only the magnifying of God's love; it was also the satisfying of God's wrath on behalf of those who believe in him. Because the Father loved us, even while we were sinners, and because Jesus also loved us, they partnered together to bring about our salvation through the sinless Son of God willingly dying the death we sinners deserve. The love of God in the Son of God rescued us from the wrath of God, without compromising the justice of God, to the glory of God.

The church has long had a precious doctrinal name for this reality, neglected today in some quarters. We introduced it in chapter 10: *propitiation*. To *propitiate* means to satisfy a divine demand, such that God becomes propitious or favorable to the one on whose behalf the sacrifice was offered. Pagans may try to *propitiate* their man-made gods, seeking favor by offering them their possessions; but the true God is made eternally favorable to his people only through Christ himself becoming a curse for us (Galatians 3:13).

That God has wrath against human sin that needs to be satisfied might be terribly offensive, if there were no Savior. More than offensive, it should be horrifying. But if the love of God has made a way—through the wondrous cross and with precious blood—then we only diminish his love when we try to lessen his wrath.

The way to let the love of God shine its brightest is not to try to mute his righteous wrath but to acknowledge it: to tremble at what we've been saved from, to stand in awe of the amazing self-giving of God's Son, and to invite others into the rescue.

—

Father, save us from the spirit of our age. May our wonder for all that Christ achieved for us at the cross not be undermined or erased by the opposing sentiments that surround us. Let the fresh air of your word, revealing the world on your terms, fill our nostrils and lungs. Banish all compromising assumptions and doctrines from our minds, and make us glory in the wonders of what you have revealed in the death of your Son for sinners. The thought of your righteous, omnipotent wrath does make us tremble, yet what a refuge we have to run to in Christ. In his wrath-removing name we pray. Amen.

Scripture reading: Galatians 3:10-14

13. A MUCH MORE EXCELLENT COVENANT

Five Contrasts with the Old

"Christ has obtained a ministry that is
as much more excellent than the old
as the covenant he mediates is better,
since it is enacted on better promises."
—Hebrews 8:6

God made the old covenant with Israel through Moses; it was an agreement about what it meant for him to be their God and they his people. Jesus did not update, renew, or renovate this covenant. The covenant he has inaugurated with his death and resurrection is not the same as the old one; nor is it an extension or adaptation of it. Rather, it is *new*. Jesus is not the latest in a long line of mediators of the same covenant. He mediates a new covenant—and he *alone* mediates this covenant.

There is now a new way of coming to God which has entirely superseded the old system with its temple building and animal sacrifices. Jesus' death can be relied upon in a way those sacrifices couldn't. As lifelong Jews, the first recipients of the epistle to the Hebrews needed to know that Christ's work for them was "for all time" (Hebrews 10:12, 14)—perfect and final. There was no need for more, and no going back to before. And why would you even want to go back if you could? Jesus, and his work, and his covenant, are *better*.

If the newness and superiority of Jesus' new covenant don't strike us with awe and wonder, perhaps it's time to get to know the old covenant better. God designed it to help us see and savor the glory of Christ, both as it foreshadows him and by way of contrast. The better we know it, the more we will stand in awe of him. And there is no better place to go to see the contrasting glory than Hebrews 9:11-14. Here, at the very heart of the letter, is a comparison of five (good) facets of the old covenant versus five (better) aspects of the new.

1. Superior Priest
Essential to God's first arrangement with his people was the appointment of mediators: *the priests* (v 6). God set aside one of Israel's twelve tribes (Levi) to serve at the altar, performing the specified rituals and duties. The priests represented God to the people, and represented the people to God.

Jesus also is a priest, and a high priest at that. Hebrews claims this from its outset (1:3; 2:17; 3:1), and then argues it at length (4:14 – 5:10; 6:20 – 8:1). However, Jesus' priesthood is of a different (and better) order. Jesus would not have been a priest under the terms of the old covenant; he was not from the priestly tribe. But as the mediator of the new covenant, his priesthood is not temporary but eternal; his sacrifice is not repeated but once for all. He is not beset with human sins and weaknesses, as other priests were, but is blameless.

2. Superior Place
The old covenant specified "an earthly place of holiness" (Hebrews 9:1): a tabernacle with two sections. The first was "the Holy Place," into which the priests went daily to perform their tasks (v 2, 6). The second was "the Most Holy Place," into which only the high priest went, and only once a year (v 3, 7). This was a *good* arrangement, enduring for a

millennium and a half, first as a tent and then as a temple. But though it was given by God, this tabernacle was still an *earthly* locale.

The place of Jesus' work is better. When Jesus had accomplished his cross-work and risen from the dead, he ascended bodily and entered into the true Holy Place ("heaven itself," v 24) "through the greater and more perfect tent (not made with hands, that is, not of this creation)" (v 11). The earthly tabernacle, as the dwelling place of God, had been just "a copy and shadow of the heavenly things" (8:5): a precursor and pointer to the true dwelling place of God. By God's design, the tabernacle was inadequate and incomplete. The place of Jesus' mediatorial work is better: he represents his people to his Father in *heaven itself.*

3. Superior Access
At the center of the old-covenant arrangement was the presence of God, portrayed in the Most Holy Place. The high priest alone was instructed to enter into that holiest of places one time each year (9:7).

Jesus' *frequency of approach* is better. He comes into the presence of his Father not once a year but *once for all.* "He entered *once for all* into the holy places" after rising from the dead (v 12). And having entered once for all, he stayed there. He remains there, dwelling continually in the presence of God. The earthly high priest *stood* while he performed his brief duties, and then left; but Jesus *sits* permanently at God's right hand on the very throne of heaven (10:11-12).

4. Superior Price
The old-covenant high priest would not dare enter the Most Holy Place without something to cover his and the people's sins. He did not enter "without taking blood, which he offers for himself and for the unintentional sins of the people" (9:7).

The blood he took was that of sacrificial animals; he entered "by means of the blood of goats and calves" (v 12).

Christ's *means of drawing near* to his Father, however, is better by far. He enters "by means of his own blood" (v 12). All along, the blood of bulls and goats had been a God-designed temporary measure. All should have known that "it is impossible for the blood of bulls and goats to take away sins" (10:4). Human death—symbolized by human blood—was the just punishment for human sin, which is cosmic treason against God Almighty.

Jesus offered *his own blood*—blood that was human, yet sinless and divine—to make the better sacrifice, the final sacrifice, for the sins of all who would trust in him. And Jesus' blood is also better, as Hebrews 9:14 adds, because it was offered voluntarily ("through the eternal Spirit [he] offered himself"), unlike the blood of animals.

5. Superior Effect

Finally, the old-covenant arrangement had an effect on the worshipers, but dealt "only with food and drink and various washings, regulations *for the body*" (v 10). It was "for the purification *of the flesh*" (v 13). However, Jesus' work has an effect on his people *inside* as well as out.

Jesus' work can "purify our conscience" (v 14) in a way that repeated animal sacrifices could not. Only Christ's new covenant can "make perfect those who draw near" (10:1)—that is, cleanse us from "any consciousness of sins" (v 2). Our sins have been dealt with totally, not merely punted forward to be reckoned with at some future time. This inward cleansing of the conscience hangs on the finality of Christ's work at the cross. The writer to the Hebrews wants to persuade us that our sense of guilt, our subjective need to be cleansed, has been dealt with objectively, decisively, and for all time—in a way that the old covenant could not, and did not attempt.

The effectiveness of Christ's work extends from the external to the internal and from the temporary to the eternal. His cross secures for us "an eternal redemption" (9:12). Through Jesus—the superior priest, who cleanses us inside and out by means of his superior blood—we are invited to approach the very throne of God himself, not just annually but weekly, daily, and at any moment (4:16).

—

Father in heaven, we approach your throne, in Christ, even now. As we set the diamond of your Son and his work against the backdrop of your first covenant with Israel, we marvel. What grace you extended to them—and now what grace upon grace you have shown us in Christ, our superior priest, who paid the superior price, in the superior place, to give us superior access, all to superior effect. We cherish your Son as our Lord and Savior and supreme treasure in all the ways you reveal his person and work to us. Captivate us afresh with his superiority over all that came before, all that is, and all that is to come. In his precious and powerful name we pray. Amen.

Scripture reading: Hebrews 9:11-22

14. GOD'S DEFINING MOMENT

How Christ Secured Our Deepest Joy

"God, who said, 'Let light shine out of darkness,'
has shone in our hearts to give the light
of the knowledge of the glory of God
in the face of Jesus Christ."
–2 Corinthians 4:6

So far, we've celebrated the wonder of the cross, the preciousness of Jesus' blood, the glory of his substitution, and the superiority of his sacrifice. Now we press deeper. What makes Jesus' cross, his spilled blood, his willing sacrifice, so compelling? What does his work achieve for us, at bottom and in the end?

The four Gospel accounts bear witness to a clear climactic "moment" in the life of Jesus of Nazareth: he died an excruciating death on the cross for sins not his own and rose three days later, vindicated. The defining days of Jesus' life—from Good Friday to Easter Sunday—have become for us God's defining moment. This is because in the death and resurrection of his Son, God secured for us three priceless realities essential for real, deep, and enduring joy.

Omnipotent Wrath Removed

We have discussed covenants already; it is worth adding more. On the night Jesus died, he took a cup, gave thanks for it, and said, "This is my *blood of the covenant*, which is poured out for many for the forgiveness of sins" (Matthew 26:28; Mark 14:24; also 1 Corinthians 11:25). In ancient times, covenants (formal agreements of any kind) were often ratified by both parties pledging their faithfulness through shedding animal blood and applying it to themselves. This portrayed the gravity of the arrangement. The ritual communicated, in essence, "May my blood likewise be shed if I do not keep the terms of this covenant." The covenant under Moses is Scripture's signature example of such a two-party covenant, with shed blood sprinkled both on the people and on the altar, which represents God (Exodus 24:3-8).

But not all covenants were inaugurated by *both* parties symbolically shedding blood. When God made a covenant with Abram, for example, God *alone* took to himself the blood of the covenant, while Abram slept (Genesis 15:7-21). In doing this, God said, in effect, *As surely as I am God, my promise to you will come to pass. It is not conditional on you. I will surely do it.*

The new covenant, inaugurated by the shedding of Jesus' blood, is like the covenant with Abram. God himself, in the person of his Son incarnate, alone spilled the blood of the covenant. It does not depend on us; there are no conditions for his choosing of us. Thus God removed his righteous wrath against his people and utterly secured, for those who are his, his eternal favor—and our everlasting joy.

New Heart Given
The removal of God's wrath is indeed grounds for rejoicing—but in order to rejoice, we need new hearts. Sin is not just a problem because it requires punishment but because it has poisoned our souls. In the new covenant, God explicitly promises a new heart. He not only removes the barrier to our lasting joy—his wrath—but also gives us the *ability* to

rejoice. Six hundred years before Christ, God said, through Jeremiah:

> *"This is the covenant that I will make with the house of Israel after those days, declares the Lord: I will put my law within them, and I will write it on their hearts." (Jeremiah 31:33; also Ezekiel 36:26)*

How amazing is Christ's purchase for us of a "new heart." Without it, we might be rescued from eternal punishment, but we would not have the ability, the heart, to experience full and lasting joy. At the cross, Jesus not only dealt with the external obstacle to our everlasting joy but also the internal. He addressed both the justice that stood against us and the corruption that was in us. And not only this, but more.

New Glory Revealed

Christ's work was not finished with wrath removed and new hearts given. To taste the fullness of joy, we need something to rejoice *in*. At the cross, in the very act of *securing* our joy, Christ himself became the most glorious *object* of our joy.

The apostle Paul writes in 2 Corinthians 4:4 that the light to which God opens the eyes of our (new) hearts is "the light of the gospel of the glory of Christ, who is the image of God." The Christian gospel—as the gospel of *the glory of Christ*—is not just the mechanism and means of obtaining our fullest and richest joy, but also the object and focus of it. Christ, the crucified God-man, lifted up in glory as he offered himself for sinners at the cross (John 8:28; 12:32), is the visible "image of the invisible God" (Colossians 1:15).

The cross is God's defining moment, as he puts forward his crucified (and risen) Son to be the conscious focus and object of our everlasting joy. Or, as Paul puts it again, just a sentence later, God "has shone in our hearts to give the light of the knowledge of *the glory of God in the face of Jesus Christ*" (2 Corinthians 4:6). Where do we look to see the glory of God in its climactic expression? In the face of his crucified (and risen) Son. We look to Jesus. We turn our eyes to the one who, in the very act of securing our joy, revealed himself to be our greatest treasure.

The Joy of the Cross

It is infinitely precious that the costly purchase of the cross includes the removal of God's righteous wrath and the provision of a new heart capable of deep and enduring joy. But the cross accomplished even more: *it brings us to God himself* (1 Peter 3:18). And as we come to God, who do we find "at the right hand of the Majesty on high" (Hebrews 1:3)? Who else but the one whom the Father has seated there with him—his own glorified Son, who has become for us the object and focus of our everlasting joy?

On its own, the cross was the most horrible, unjust event in the history of the world. But Christian, in your pursuit of joy, do not be tempted to avoid the cross. We cannot. Rather, we turn precisely to the cross, seeing how fitting it was for God, in the world of sorrow and death we inhabit, to secure our joy through the gruesome death of his own Son.

In the cross, we find God's defining moment. This was when he removed the ultimate obstacle to our joy and secured for us a new heart of joy. This was when, in the very act of purchasing our joy, he *became* the most glorious object of our joy.

———

Father, we stand in awe of your Son. Not only is he your eternal, divine Son made man, and not only did he go to the cross for us—as your defining moment—but in doing so he became the very crucified and risen Christ you made our hearts to focus on for ever-deepening and eternally enduring joy. We cherish the cross-work of your Son, not only because of what it does for us but because of who it shows him to be for us. Oh, we want to know him more! We long to know and enjoy and have Jesus more as our own. More than all he gives, we want him. Draw us closer to him as we go deeper in his work and grow in our admiration for him. In his dear name we pray. Amen.

Scripture reading: 2 Corinthians 3:12 – 4:6

15. GET TO THE CROSS
AND NEVER LEAVE

"You are in Christ Jesus,
who became to us wisdom from God,
righteousness and sanctification
and redemption."
–1 Corinthians 1:30

We began Part 2 by marveling at the "wondrous cross." There we rehearsed 1 Corinthians 1:23-24 and the folly—and wisdom—of Christ crucified. Now we finish Part 2 with 1 Corinthians 1:30 and the ongoing, daily relevance of the cross in the Christian life. Before we move to focus on the resurrection, let's first ponder the sense in which Christians never "move on" from the cross.

Scottish pastor and poet Horatius Bonar (1808-1889) wrote in 1864 in the book *God's Way of Holiness*:

> *The secret of a believer's holy walk is his continual*
> *recurrence to the blood of the Surety, and his daily*
> *[communion] with a crucified and risen Lord. All*
> *divine life, and all precious fruits of it, pardon,*
> *peace, and holiness, spring from the cross. All fancied*
> *sanctification which does not arise wholly from the*
> *blood of the cross is nothing better than Pharisaism.*
> *If we would be holy, we must get to the cross, and*
> *dwell there; else, notwithstanding all our labour,*
> *diligence, fasting, praying, and good works, we shall*

be yet void of real sanctification, destitute of those humble, gracious tempers which accompany a clear view of the cross.

Bonar's charge cuts painfully across the grain of our day, and his antiquated language (once we have understood it) may provide a fresh wind from another century to blow through the stale air of our subtle assumptions. Let's linger here and see.

All Springs from the Cross?

What is the biblical support for the claim that all true holiness, and all genuine good acts, "spring from the cross"? For the early Christians, the crucifixion of Christ was not simply a singular event. It quickly became, as God's defining moment, part of his identity, and theirs.

It already served as a kind of identifying descriptor of our Lord in the immediate aftermath of his resurrection, as the angel spoke to the women at the empty tomb: "Do not be afraid, for I know that you seek *Jesus who was crucified.* He is not here, for he has risen" (Matthew 28:5-6; so also Mark 16:6).

Fifty days later, at Pentecost, Peter declared, "Let all the house of Israel therefore know for certain that God has made him both Lord and Christ, this *Jesus whom you crucified*" (Acts 2:36). He told the council that he had performed miracles "by the name of Jesus Christ of Nazareth, *whom you crucified,* whom God raised from the dead" (Acts 4:10). "Crucified," as an identifying marker of Jesus, came into its own in the ministry of the apostle Paul, who wrote that, in his preaching, "Jesus Christ was publicly portrayed as *crucified*" (Galatians 3:1). Christians, he insisted, "preach *Christ crucified*" (1 Corinthians 1:23).

The cross is not simply a component of the gospel message that tips nonbelievers into the kingdom through faith. The early church saw that the cross was "the most astonishing act of *divine self-disclosure* that has ever occurred" (D.A. Carson, *The Cross and Christian Ministry*, p 16). It reveals to us God himself: his ways in the world (wisdom), how to get right with him (righteousness), how to be genuinely holy (sanctification), and what it means to be bought back from the world (redemption). Which is why Paul went on to say, "I decided to know nothing among you except *Jesus Christ and him crucified*" (1 Corinthians 2:2)—not because his preaching was narrow and constrained but because the cross is so deeply significant and all-pervasive.

Fancied Sanctification vs. Real

In 1 Corinthians 1:30, Paul says that this crucified Christ "became to us ... *sanctification*," or literally, *holiness* (Greek *hagiasmos*). To come to faith in him who was crucified is to be decisively set apart from this world and its patterns, from sin and its reign; and then to be progressively set apart as we grow in grace through faith in him and by the power of his Spirit. This is *real sanctification* for the Christian, both given to us and worked in us. We have, at once, the gift of Christ's holiness, and with it a new *position* in the eyes of God; and then, over time, new *progress*, as his holiness grows and takes root in us. Bonar warns us of an imposter: a "fancied sanctification" that "does not arise wholly from the blood of the cross."

For Christians, true worship and "real sanctification" not only flow from the purchase of the cross, but also draw strength from conscious faith in the crucified Christ. We know our former selves to be *crucified* with him (Romans 6:6). "I have been crucified with Christ," Paul says. "It is no longer I who live, but Christ who lives in me. And the life I now live in the flesh I live by faith in the Son of God, who loved me and gave himself for me" (Galatians 2:20). Paul's holiness—his spiritual growth, his acts of love, his accomplishing anything of spiritual, eternal good—was not due to

him, sinner that he was. Rather, it was because of the crucified one, in whom Paul now lived by faith.

The Secret?

What about us? If we are to grow and mature as Christians, and if we are to live holy lives, we too must "get to
the cross, and dwell there." Bonar claims, "The secret of a
believer's holy walk is his *continual recurrence* to the blood of
the Surety, and his daily [communion] with a crucified and
risen Lord."

Here "the Surety" is a reference to the cross as an ob-
jective event and fact: God's demonstration, in history, of
his gracious heart toward his people, and the guarantee of
his everlasting favor. Bonar commends "continual recurrence"—ongoing return—to the cross in daily communion
with our *crucified* and risen Lord.

Neither Paul nor Bonar then turns to prescribe for us what
"continual" and "constant" *getting to the cross* must look like
in every time, place, season, and life. But Christians in every
time and place can benefit from asking themselves: *Am I
indeed getting to the cross?* Do I really dwell there, through
faith? What would it take for me to do so? How *constant*
and how *continual* our approach is may vary, but we either
"get to the cross, and dwell there" or not. And our holiness
is either real or fancied.

Bonar does mention one general indicator: "daily." And I
can testify that daily is not too often. God will see to it that
our hearts never tire of knowing our Lord as crucified for us.
Having lived with this old, old truth now for almost twenty
years, I can say it has never grown close to stale. It has only
ever become sweeter.

Father, as we now move to focus on the resurrection, we dare not "move on" from the cross. Christ crucified is our life. Him we proclaim—to our world, to our neighbors, to our family, and to our own souls. Work this "secret" in us in our continual return to Jesus' blood, in daily communion with our crucified and risen Lord. May all our life spring from the cross. Make our holiness real, not fancied. Get us daily to the cross and keep us there. In Jesus' name we pray. Amen.

Scripture reading: 1 Corinthians 1:26 – 2:5

Part 3

HIS TRIUMPH

"The Lord has risen indeed!"
—Luke 24:34

16. HIS HEART BEATS

"You were ransomed from the futile ways
inherited from your forefathers,
not with perishable things such as silver or gold,
but with the precious blood of Christ."
—1 Peter 1:18-19

Now we turn to the resurrection of Christ. First, consider with me those very first moments of resurrection life, and how precious is the beating heart of the Son of God.

In taking our flesh *and blood* and becoming man, the Son acquired, along with his truly human body and reasoning soul, an actual human heart—not the spiritual heart of uncreated deity but one like the one pumping, right now, in your body, keeping the blood of life flowing through your veins.

His Human Heart

One marvel of human gestation is that our hearts begin to beat only three weeks after conception. Only weeks after the angel appeared and announced to his mother, "Behold, you will conceive in your womb and bear a son, and you shall call his name Jesus" (Luke 1:31), the human heart of the Son of God began to beat. Then for nine more months, his heart grew larger and stronger. And for more than three decades, moment by moment, one precious beat after another, the human heart of the Son of God pumped. Each beat pumped life-giving blood in the one in whom is life. Each beat sent "the precious blood of Christ" coursing through the human body of one without spot or blemish (1 Peter 1:19).

Never has more hung on a human pulse. And that heart did beat, without pause, from the womb, throughout his childhood, to adulthood. As he learned to walk and talk, and as he learned to read. As he asked questions of his elders at the temple when he was twelve. And as he learned to work with his hands and labor as a carpenter. His heart beat as he rested and slept, and its rate rose as he moved about Nazareth: walking, running, lifting, navigating up and down steps and hills.

On average it beat almost five thousand times each hour, and more than 100,000 times each day—and in all, more than 42 million times each year. Each beat upheld by the hand of his Father, like each beat of your heart.

His Heart Stops

Yet, on that singularly terrible Friday—the one we've now learned to call Good—his human heart finally stopped.

Pilate washed his hands, saying, "I am innocent of this man's blood" (Matthew 27:24). They scourged Jesus. How close did his heart come to stopping as lash 38 landed, further tearing open his lacerated back—and then 39? When he shouldered his own crossbeam, wearing a crown of thorns, how did his heart endure? Then they nailed him there for his final six hours until, at last, in agony, he could no longer breathe, and the human heart of the Son of God stopped.

They pierced his side to confirm he was dead, and took his body down. For Friday night, and all day Saturday, and into the early hours of Sunday, there his body lay, dead. His lungs and nostrils did not breathe. He had no pulse. His heart did not beat.

His Heart Beats

Have you ever pondered those world-altering moments that Sunday morning inside the tomb? His eleven disciples, the women, the soldiers, and Pilate were sealed on the outside of the stone. But what mattered most, the body of Christ—and his human heart—lay inside.

Imagine that first instant, as the angels saw it from heaven, when his cold, lifeless heart began to beat again. Was his human body transfigured in a moment, as God had transfigured it for the eyes of his disciples on the mountain (Matthew 17:2; Mark 9:2-3)? Or, in divine patience, did God slowly produce the first taste of the harvest to come—glorifying his flesh, gently warming his heart, and then, for the first time, making it beat again, now with an unstoppable rhythm, one that will march on without end?

So Beat Our Hearts

Now Jesus' glorified human heart will never again cease to beat. It pumps the blood of eternal life through his human veins—and for all his people. Resurrected, he ascended, in our human flesh and blood, to heaven. He pioneered our way into the very presence of God as our fellow human and sat down, with all authority, on heaven's throne at the right hand of his Father. And one day soon, we will see him as he is, and be like him (1 John 3:2).

Jesus our Lord has "entered once for all into the holy places, not by means of the blood of goats and calves but by means of his own blood, thus securing an eternal redemption" for his people (Hebrews 9:12). Even now, "in him we have redemption through his blood, the forgiveness of our trespasses, according to the riches of his grace" (Ephesians 1:7). In him, we are "the church of God, which he obtained with his own blood" (Acts 20:28)—that is, "the precious blood of Christ" (1 Peter 1:19).

Now, in Christ, our hearts beat. He has opened the eyes of our hearts to see "the immeasurable greatness of his power toward us who believe" (Ephesians 1:18-19). Even as we know that our present physical hearts will one day stop, as his did, so he has promised us that we, like him, will rise.

How precious is the beating, blood-pumping heart of the Son of God? Infinitely precious.

—

Father, how amazing to ponder all that hung, and hangs, on the precious blood and beating heart of your divine-human Son. What a marvel that he, God himself, the eternal Son, took our own flesh and blood, gave himself to the sacrificial spilling of his blood, and rose in triumph to bring us with him. We praise your Son not only for the demonstration of his love as he gave his life for us at the cross, but also for the life and power and victory we have in his life as risen. And so we have him—not just his work—as our great treasure. In his risen and triumphant name we pray. Amen.

Scripture reading: John 20:1-10

17. HE IS RISEN INDEED

"'O death, where is your victory?
O death, where is your sting?'
The sting of death is sin, and the power of sin is the law.
But thanks be to God, who gives us the victory
through our Lord Jesus Christ."
—1 Corinthians 15:55–57

God made music for this. He gave us voices to sing this truth. Pitch and cadence, rhythm and rhyme, melody and harmony—he wired the world, and created humanity, to break into song together over the one victory that is almost too good for words: *Jesus is alive.*

So we play strings and pound drums. We sing with gusto. We write new songs. This news is too great for whispers. This truth too magnificent for indoor voices. This message too astonishing for us to keep our cool. And when it seems that our hearts are beginning to burst for joy, here we find why he gave us music. He made us for this song: *he is alive!*

He Is Not Here

The women who came early on Sunday morning to his tomb were the first to find out. They had suffered the longest days and nights of their lives on Friday and Saturday. They had seen his agony and ignominy. They watched his blood pour out. They witnessed the weight of the curse on him. They saw the sky go dark. They heard his cry of abandonment, then his prayer, and then his final breath.

For two days, they had sobbed their eyes dry and mourned their voices raw. Now the Sabbath had passed, and their grief continued as they brought spices to anoint his body. They felt the ground shake (Matthew 28:2). They found the stone rolled away, but not his body (Luke 24:2-3). Confusion and numbness. Then everything changed with that word from the angel: "He is not here, but has risen" (v 6).

Fear and Great Joy

This was news too great for a simple, predictable response. We're told, "They departed quickly from the tomb with *fear and great joy*" (Matthew 28:8). Fear and great joy together.

They feared because of the raw power of resurrection. Nothing but the power of God himself was on display. God himself. The sheer strength that was shown in triumphing over the final enemy was enough to make the most courageous shake. Omnipotent power had been unleashed, and it had shattered the seemingly impenetrable skull of death itself.

And the women had great joy, because this power was on their side. Better, they were on his side. The one whom they loved was alive. More alive than they had ever dreamed. The one they trusted and followed, and believed in, not only had been shown to be true, but was alive—alive to hear and see and touch. He was—and is—alive to know and enjoy. Forever.

Because He Lives

What Jesus has accomplished for us in his sacrificial death at the cross is so amazing, so remarkable, so world-changing, that it's easy to understand why we have made this emblem so prominent in the church. But with such a fitting emphasis on this spectacular event at Calvary, it can be easy to overlook other equally important events. One regular casualty is Jesus' resurrection. We have Easter Sunday set aside for that, but during the rest of the year, it can be easy to unthinkingly play down the empty tomb, or at least miss this essential truth: not only did Jesus once live and die and rise, but today he *lives*.

For the Christian, just as important as Jesus' bloody cross is his empty tomb. Because it means he lives.

My Savior Lives

The apostle Paul doesn't leave any doubt about the importance of the resurrection when he writes in 1 Corinthians 15:

> *"If Christ has not been raised, then our preaching is in vain and your faith is in vain ... If Christ has not been raised, your faith is futile and you are still in your sins ... If in Christ we have hope in this life only, we are of all people most to be pitied."*
>
> *(v 14-19)*

That Jesus died means that in him our sin has received its just punishment; that he lives means that we have in him the righteousness God requires. That he died means we have forgiveness; that he lives means we have righteousness. He "was delivered up for our trespasses and raised for our justification" (Romans 4:25).

That Jesus died means he has offered up, as our great high priest, his great sacrifice on our behalf. "By a single offering he has perfected for all time those who are being sanctified" (Hebrews 10:14). That he lives means he now unceasingly intercedes for us at his Father's right hand. "He is able to save to the uttermost those who draw near to God through him, since he always lives to make intercession for them" (Hebrews 7:25).

Our Living, Loving Lord

That Jesus died means he has demonstrated climactically

in history his love for his church. As the apostle Paul says, he "loved me and gave himself for me" (Galatians 2:20), because "God shows his love for us in that while we were still sinners, Christ died for us" (Romans 5:8). That he lives means that not only has he shown his love for us in the past, but that he loves us today. As surely as he lives, he loves us.

That Jesus lives means that our best days are not behind us but ahead; that our great hope is not some mere hero of the past but the living Lord of the universe; that our faith is not dead but unites us to an active Savior, Treasure, and Friend.

It is an infinitely precious thing to say not just that Jesus died, but that *he lives.*

Join the Chorus

What the women at first did not understand, now we know: joy has triumphed over sorrow. Christ, through death, has destroyed the one who had the power of death (Hebrews 2:14). Death is swallowed up in victory (1 Corinthians 15:54).

It is too great for mere speech. There must be song. Indeed there is. We join the chorus with the apostle Paul, who writes about the resurrection not just in ordinary prose but as a song, quoting from the prophet Hosea:

> *"O death, where is your victory? O death, where is your sting?" (1 Corinthians 15:55)*

Christ is risen. He is alive. How can we not sing?

———

Father, yes, indeed, your Son is alive, and that changes everything. In him, the risen Christ, our best days are not behind us but ahead. In the living Christ, our great hope is not some mere hero of the past but the living Lord of the universe. Holy Father, in our cherishing of the old, rugged cross, may we never minimize that grandeur of the resurrection. Our everything hangs on the risen Christ. We could not—we would not—have his work without having him. Awaken us afresh in these days to the risen, indestructible life of Christ, our living Lord. In his name we pray. Amen.

Scripture reading: 1 Corinthians 15:50-58

18. HE CANNOT BE STOPPED

God raised him up, loosing the pangs of death,
because it was not possible for him to be held by it.
—Acts 2:24

Confused as his disciples may have been as word spread that he was *alive*, they were thrown for another dramatic and disorienting loop as they pondered what it all meant.

Long had they known that, ordinary as he looked, Jesus was no ordinary man. But the pieces had come together one at a time, over some time. Water to wine. Multiplying loaves to feed thousands. Calming the storm. Restoring sight to the blind. A paralysed man walks. A little girl, declared dead, rises. Lazarus comes out of his tomb at Jesus' word. And, on top of it all, his stunning teaching. They marveled at his words. No one spoke like this man (John 7:46). The picture was becoming clearer and clearer. This indeed must be God's long-promised Messiah. *Might this even be, somehow, in some mind-blowing way, God himself among us?*

Then, just as the picture had appeared to come together, it seemed to fall apart, crashing to the ground, all in less than 24 hours. Jesus had been stopped. He was arrested and tried with shocking injustice. How could it be that such a man would be sentenced to death, nailed to a cross, and executed as the worst of criminals?

Then came the two longest nights of their lives.

Then he was *alive*.

Unstoppable Plan

It's not as though Jesus hadn't told them what was coming. They simply had been unable to take it in. Their understanding of what "Messiah" meant had assumed a straight path to glory, not this convoluted one. But he had warned them, "The Son of Man is about to be delivered into the hands of men, and they will kill him, and he will be raised on the third day" (Matthew 17:22-23). None of it caught Jesus off guard. He knew it was coming, and he had set his face toward Jerusalem (Luke 9:51), as a man walking out the details of a plan he himself had made.

"No one takes [my life] from me," he had said, "but I lay it down of my own accord. I have authority to lay it down, and I have authority to take it up again" (John 10:18). Now he was alive, and this confirmed it for all time. He *did* have such authority—not only to lay his life down when he chose and as he chose, but the authority to take it up again.

Finally, his disciples would realize that he was indeed unstoppable. On the Emmaus road, he opened their eyes, and opened to them the Scriptures (Luke 24:26-27, 31-32, 45-46). Even locked doors could not keep him out (John 20:19). Thomas, shown mercy despite his doubts, could put his fingers on Jesus' nailed-scarred hands and side (John 20:25, 27), seeing and touching the evidence: Christ could not be stopped.

His Unstoppable People

His resurrection from the dead declares once and for all that Jesus is unstoppable. The power the risen, glorified Christ now wields is "the power of an indestructible life" (Hebrews 7:16). In fact, as Peter came to know, and to preach at Pentecost, "God raised him up, loosing the pangs of death, because *it was not possible for him to be held by it*" (Acts 2:24). As Paul wrote to the Romans, "We know that Christ, being raised from the dead, will never die again; death no longer has dominion over him" (Romans 6:9). His disciples could not stop their mouths. Jesus was alive, and now it was their unceasing joy to declare it.

But the resurrection of Christ declares even more for those of us who are joined to him by faith. Not only is *he* unstoppable—*so are we*. "I am the resurrection and the life," he says. "Whoever believes in me … shall never die" (John 11:25-26). What is the power at work in us, even now—we who have faith in him? We know "the immeasurable greatness of [God's] power toward us who believe, according to the working of his great might that he worked in Christ *when he raised him from the dead*" (Ephesians 1:19-20).

Wars, earthquakes, famines, pestilences, and terrors will come (Luke 21:10-11). Christ's people will be despised, opposed, insulted, and persecuted (v 12). Some will be put to death (v 16). And yet, he promises, "Not a hair of your head will perish" (v 18). Christ's people cannot be stopped—even in earthly death. Death has become gain (Philippians 1:21), because Christ has conquered, and we are eternally safe in him. As his disciples, how can we not delight to spread the news?

Unstoppable God

Christ's resurrection, then, is a tribute to our unstoppable God. Just when it looked like maybe God could be stopped, he held his breath, patiently counted to three, and then breathed again the breath of life into the nostrils of his Son. Christ's heart began to beat. He opened his eyes. He made his bed, folding the grave clothes. He rolled back the stone, and he walked away in patient, calm, unstoppable power.

The empty tomb is God's great declaration in history, and refrain in our hearts, and announcement to the nations, that he indeed cannot be stopped.

Father in heaven, we declare ourselves to be gladly yours, our unstoppable God. We put our hands over our mouths in awe and wonder, to consider what you've drawn us into with the resurrection of your Son. What a marvel to not only see it, and admire it, but to experience it, in the resurrection of our dead hearts, and in the very triumph of your Son, into which he welcomes his church. Father, be unstoppable in us, in smiting sin and chasing away the darkness, and be unstoppable in our world, in and through your church, to the glory of your risen Son. In the mercy and might of his name we pray. Amen.

Scripture reading: Acts 2:14-24

19. HE IS EXALTED

The Ascended and Seated Christ

As they were looking on, he was lifted up,
and a cloud took him out of their sight.
—Acts 1:9

What does it mean when we say that Jesus is "exalted" at God's right hand?

Perhaps you've thought of this in terms of our exalting him. We exalt him in our praises. As we sing over and over again in one popular chorus, "I exalt thee." We do exalt Jesus when we declare his worth, and speak of his greatness, and sing words of praise. He is exalted in our declarations of his worth. A central aspect of what it means to be a Christian is that Christ is our Lord, and we exalt him in our worship and with our lives.

But when we say that Jesus is "exalted," the first and most important truth to draw attention to isn't that we exalt him but that God exalts him: welcoming him to sit, as king, on the very throne of heaven. As Philippians 2:9 says, "*God has highly exalted him* and bestowed on him the name that is above every name."

First God exalts him; then we follow suit.

Jesus Ascended
But let's take one step back, to forge the critical link between Jesus' resurrection and his exaltation at his Father's right hand:

the ascension. For centuries, the Christian church has marked the fortieth day after Easter as Ascension Day, in remembrance of Jesus' bodily ascent to heaven. The number forty is based on Acts 1:3: "He presented himself alive to them after his suffering by many proofs, appearing to them *during forty days* and speaking about the kingdom of God." For forty days, he stayed with them, ate with them, gave them his final instructions and encouragements, and told them not to leave Jerusalem until he had poured out on them, from heaven, the new-covenant fullness of the Holy Spirit. Then, as they looked on, "he was lifted up"—he ascended—"and a cloud took him out of their sight" (Acts 1:9).

The doctrine of the ascension is not a truth that the recent history of theology has been apt to emphasize, but it is essential to the gospel. Wisely did the ancient church confess, in such short space, not only that…

> *he was conceived by the Holy Spirit, born of the*
> *Virgin Mary, suffered under Pontius Pilate, was*
> *crucified, died, and was buried; on the third day he*
> *rose again…*

but also that…

> *he ascended into heaven, he is seated at the right*
> *hand of the Father, and he will come again to judge*
> *the living and the dead.*

Jesus' ascension into the presence of God gets all that he accomplished "down here" to count for us "up there" with God. Jesus is, right now, in glorified humanity on the throne of the universe, wielding "all authority in heaven and on earth" (Matthew 28:18). He didn't dissolve into the sky or float away; he ascended to heaven to reign over all. He is not just our suffering servant who came and died and rose triumphant, but our actively ruling, actively conquering King.

Without Jesus' ascension, there would be no true access to God, no full measure of the Spirit, and no great salvation. The ascension is a link in the chain of salvation as essential as Jesus' life, death, and resurrection.

Jesus Seated

After his ascension, then, comes his *session*—his taking his seat on heaven's throne.

The whole first chapter of Hebrews is a kind of celebration of the Father exalting the Son upon his return to heaven. It pictures the climactic coronation ceremony of the universe: the Son, having ascended to heaven in his resurrection body, proceeds into the very presence of his Father and the angels, and—in fulfillment of ages of regal prophecies—ascends to the throne and sits down. He has accomplished his work of redemption.

As the divine second Person of the Trinity, the Son has always been worthy of exaltation as God. From the beginning, he was the one "appointed the heir of all things, through whom also [God] created the world. He is the radiance of the glory of God and the exact imprint of his nature, and he upholds the universe by the word of his power" (Hebrews 1:2-3).

But something new happened when the Son took our humanity and was born in Bethlehem. Now he was not just God but the God-man—always fully God and now also fully man. He started life as a human from scratch, from the very bottom: as an infant, born in humility.

Yet he showed himself worthy of heights greater than any human in history—not just in his holiness and freedom from sin, but decisively in the love with which he died sacrificially for sins that were ours, not his. As the perfect image of God (Colossians 1:15; 2 Corinthians 4:4), he fulfilled the very destiny of man. Now Jesus is worthy not only as God, but also as man. And so, "after making purification for sins, *he sat down* at the right hand of the Majesty on high, having become as much superior to angels as the name he has inherited is more excellent than theirs" (Hebrews 1:3-4).

Thunderclap of Exaltation

He was always the divine Son. But by virtue of accomplishing his sacrificial work, he was, now as man, "declared to be the Son of God in power according to the Spirit of holiness by his resurrection from the dead" (Romans 1:4). In one sense, all authority was always his as God. But in another sense, as man, now he was able to say, "All authority in heaven and on earth has been given to me" (Matthew 28:18).

God now has crowned him King of all kings, at the very apex of the universe, not just as God but as man. The man Christ Jesus sits in the very seat of God, and "he must reign until he has put all his enemies under his feet" (1 Corinthians 15:25).

This is what it means, first and foremost, that "he is exalted." He rose. He ascended. And the Father highly exalted his Son to the very highest of places. The Ancient of Days has acknowledged the fullness and completeness of the work of his Son, the God-man, and has raised him to the throne at his right hand.

And in response to this thunderclap of God exalting his Son, we chime in with our whispers of exaltation. God has exalted his Son to the highest of heights, that we might catch a glimpse of such glory and echo our exaltation in our words and songs of praise.

Father in heaven, we do join with you in exalting your Son. You have exalted him decisively, to heaven's throne, and now we exalt him in our praise, in spoken and sung and lived-out echoes of his majesty and worth. Not only is he risen, but he reigns. He ascended. He took his seat. And you crowned him Lord of all and wield all your divine power and authority through him— our brother—on heaven's throne. In his marvelous and majestic name we pray. Amen.

Scripture reading: Acts 1:1-11

20. HIS REIGN HAS BEGUN

Christ as Sovereign and Judge

"Behold, with the clouds of heaven there came
one like a son of man, and he came to
the Ancient of Days and was presented before him.
And to him was given dominion and glory and a kingdom."
—Daniel 7:13-14

"**A**ncient of Days" appears as a name for God in only one chapter of the Bible. But that chapter, Daniel 7, is no obscure vision. In fact, that passage also gives us the title Jesus used more often than any other to refer to himself: *the Son of Man*. Written centuries before Christ came, this chapter also gives us a glimpse into the glory of Christ's resurrection and ascension into heaven.

We have moved from those first moments of his beating resurrection heart, to the telling of the message to his disciples, to the demonstration of his risen invincibility. In the last chapter, we traced the path of his ascension from earth to heaven, and his sitting down as the universe's King. Now, before we return to his great coronation, we turn to an ancient prophecy, fulfilled as the risen Christ strode toward heaven's throne.

Some five and a half centuries before Christ, God gave this vision to the prophet Daniel in a dream, while he lived in exile in Babylon. Three times Daniel tells us that it was night (v 2, 7, 13), to indicate the nature of the vision: not a precise script but a distant prophetic glimpse of a man coming to heaven's throne to receive all authority. Shadowy as it was, Daniel wrote down the sum of what he saw (v 1). It has consoled and inspired God's people now for millennia, especially in times of anxiety and alarm.

Evil Terrorizes God's People

First, Daniel sees four great beasts come up out of the sea (v 3), each more threatening than the one before. The first is like a lion, with eagles' wings. Then another, like a bear, devouring flesh. A third is like a leopard with wings and four heads. Finally comes "a fourth beast, terrifying and dreadful and exceedingly strong" (v 7). It is "different from all the beasts that were before it" (v 7, 19, 23) in its strength and in the terror it inspires—devouring "the whole earth" (v 23). This sequence represents the escalation of evil as worldly powers rise up against God and his people. It not only played out among ancient nations—from Babylon to Persia to Greece to Rome—but continues in our own fallen age.

The final beast has ten horns, a symbol of great power, and Daniel says, "There came up among them another horn, a little one" with "a mouth speaking great things" (v 8). This is perhaps a final great ruler, who turns his arrogant tongue against God and his people. He will "speak words against the Most High," the prophet says, "and shall wear out the saints of the Most High" (v 25). His verbal threats give rise to acts of persecution that seem successful for a time. He "made war with the saints and prevailed over them"—that is, "until the Ancient of Days came" (v 21-22).

The Ancient of Days Judges

Daniel then sees that "thrones were placed"—this is a judgment scene—and "the Ancient of Days took his seat" (v 9), presiding over all the nations—and all of history—to deliver his binding verdict. He far surpasses the strength, authority, extent, and duration of all the world's greatest dynasties, ancient and modern. This is God himself, who takes his seat as Judge of all he has made.

He is clothed in white to reflect his utter purity; his hair, like pure wool, reveals his boundless wisdom, proven over endless ages. He is surrounded by fire which streams forth from his throne, flashing his power to conquer any challenger. Now the evil powers face the reckoning for their rebellion. The fourth and greatest beast is immediately destroyed (v 11; also v 26), and the arrogant mouth silenced.

However long the wait may seem to his people, and however impatient they become, God will act with justice, in his perfect timing. He will destroy the wicked and silence the loudest of hostile mouths.

The Son of Man Emerges

Then comes a remarkable turn. The Ancient of Days gives sovereign rulership to a divine-human figure called "the son of man."

Daniel sees "one like a son of man, and he came to the Ancient of Days and was presented before him" (v 13). Mark this: the Ancient of Days *transfers his own dominion* over all the nations to this "son of man"—an everlasting dominion, we're told, that will not pass away (v 14). The son of man rules over all, and his kingdom will not end. Though human, he far surpasses any other king. No other past, present, or future human sovereign has reigned, or will ever reign, without end. This is the reign into which Christ entered when he sat down at God's right hand.

The Saints Join Him

Finally, this vision becomes amazingly personal for those of us who call ourselves God's people, his holy ones, his saints. Our God, the Ancient of Days, has the wisdom, authority, and power to judge the nations—and *we are included*. Not just as spectators. The people of God play a stunning part in the culmination of history, which has begun in Christ and yet is still to come.

Verse 18 makes the first declaration, still future for us: "*The saints* of the Most High shall receive the kingdom and possess the kingdom forever, forever and ever." The eternal, divine kingdom does not only belong to the Son of Man; now also, through him, it will belong to all God's people. Evil will be allowed to make war on the saints, but only "*until* ... the time [comes] when the saints [possess] the kingdom" (v 22). In the end, to our astonishment, "the kingdom and the dominion and the greatness of the kingdoms under the whole heaven shall be given"—to whom? To us, the saints (v 27). To the church.

Long has the Ancient of Days intended this vision in Daniel 7 to give great hope to his people, come what may. Not only because of his majestic transcendence and unsurpassed power, but also because of his nearness to his saints. He will sit to judge, and he will give us his everlasting kingdom.

The resurrected Christ, who is the Son of Man, has ascended to his throne to receive power. It may yet be centuries before the church is fully rescued and the vision is complete. Or perhaps only years, or days. Seated on heaven's throne, his next great move will be to rescue the saints.

———

Father in heaven, Ancient of Days, what can we even begin to say about the lavish and ceaseless grace that is ours in Christ? Not only will your Son, the Son of Man, judge the world with equity and protect his people from the wicked, but he will make us judges with him. He will draw us into his reign, bringing us with him to his very throne. This will be a grace and glory past finding out. A grace and glory that will take all eternity to discover. So, quiet our restless hearts. Satisfy our thirsty souls. Feed our empty stomachs in this world, as we reach in faith to receive these stunning promises in your Son. In his humbled and exalted name we pray. Amen.

Scripture reading: Daniel 7:9-14

21. HE SAT DOWN

The Great Coronation in Heaven

After making purification for sins,
he sat down at the right hand of the Majesty on high.
—Hebrews 1:3

Imagine that moment when Jesus first sat down on heaven's throne.

Having taken on our full flesh and blood, lived among us, died sacrificially for us, and risen in triumph, defeating sin and death, he ascended to heaven, pioneering our way, as human, into the very presence of God his Father. Then Jesus stepped forward toward the throne. All heaven—angels and saints, living creatures and elders (Revelation 4:4-7)—was transfixed by history's great coronation: a ceremony so glorious that even the most extravagant of earthly coronations can barely reflect it.

Most of us today don't even have the categories for the kind of pomp and circumstance that accompanied coronations in the ancient world. We've never witnessed an entire kingdom harness all its collective wealth and skill to put on a once-in-a-generation tribute to the glory of its leader. The extravagance communicates the importance of the person and his or her position. Royal weddings, no doubt, have their splendor; but the ascending of a new monarch to the throne, and that solemn moment of placing on his head the crown that signaled his power, was without equal.

And yet all the majesty of history's most grandiose coronations has now been dwarfed by the heavenly finale. Now we see that the greatest of earthly ceremonies was but the faintest of shadows, anticipating this climactic moment.

Crown Him Lord of All

The first chapter of Hebrews gives us a glimpse into this coronation of Christ, this moment when the God-man was formally crowned Lord of all. First, the scene is set: "After making purification for sins, he sat down at the right hand of the Majesty on high" (Hebrews 1:3).

Then Hebrews quotes from Psalm 2, which was a psalm of coronation for the ancient people of God: "You are my Son," God says to the new king of Israel; "today I have begotten you" (Hebrews 1:5). It was on the day of his ascension to the throne that the new ruler of God's people formally became God's "son" in this sense—serving as his official representative to his people. The coronation was the day, so to speak, that God begat the human king as his son and lord over his people. For Jesus, it was the day when his Father formally installed him as the risen God-man on the throne of the universe.

To Him All Majesty Ascribe

Next, verse 6 mentions "when [God] brings the firstborn into the world." What world? This is not a reference to the incarnation but to Jesus' return to heaven, following his ascension. Hebrews 2:5 clarifies by referencing "the world to come, *of which we are speaking.*" In other words, "the world" in view in Hebrews 1 is not our earthly, temporal age, into which Jesus came through birth in Bethlehem. Rather, the world into which God brings his firstborn here is the heavenly realm, what is to us "the world to come": heaven itself, into which Jesus ascended following his earthly mission.

The setting is indeed the great enthronement of the King of kings. And as Jesus enters heaven itself and advances to its ruling seat, God announces, "Let all God's angels worship him" (1:6). Him: God *and man* in one spectacular person.

Originally God made man "a little lower than the heavenly beings" (Psalm 8:5). But now the angelic hosts of heaven *worship him*, "the man Christ Jesus" (1 Timothy 2:5). So great is this man, as a genuine member of our race, that he not only eclipses and bypasses the race of angels, but, in doing so, he brings his people with him. No redeemer has arisen for fallen angels. "Surely it is not angels that he helps, but he helps the offspring of Abraham" (Hebrews 2:16). In Christ, angels no longer look *down* to humanity but *up*. And we now experience firsthand "things into which angels long to look" (1 Peter 1:12).

This new King of the universe is indeed fully man and fully God, and addressed as such (quoting Psalm 45): "Your throne, O God, is forever and ever" (Hebrews 1:8). Verse 12 (echoing Psalm 102) restates the glory—"Your years will have no end"—which is the ultimate expression of that famous declaration, "Long live the king!" (1 Samuel 10:24; 2 Samuel 16:16; 1 Kings 1:25, 34; 2 Kings 11:12; 2 Chronicles 23:11).

Bring Forth the Royal Diadem

Finally, the grand finale sounds the great oracle of Psalm 110, which has lingered in the background since the mention of Jesus sitting down in Hebrews 1:3. Again the Father speaks: "Sit at my right hand until I make your enemies a footstool for your feet" (v 13). For generations and centuries, the people of God had waited for the day in which great David's greater son, his Lord, would ascend to the throne and hear these sacred words from God himself. Then, at long last, captured for us in the vision of Hebrews 1, the great enigmatic dream of Psalm 110 is finally realized.

Having finished the work his Father gave him to accomplish, God's own Son (not merely David's) has ascended to the throne—not a throne on earth but the throne of heaven. The Father himself has crowned him King of all the universe. He has called forth the royal diadem and crowned him King of every family, every tribe, every nation: King of all time and space and history.

We who call him King and Lord will gather one day with all the angels and saints to fall at his feet. Even now, he gives us the dignity of participating in heaven's coronation ceremony as we crown him Lord both with our praises and with our glad obedience. We crown him Lord through daily lives of continual praise (Hebrews 13:15) and as we gather weekly with our new kindred and tribe in worship (2:12).

The glorious enthronement of Christ has not ended but continues. We see it now and experience it by faith, and we participate in it with our praises. And one day soon, with all his redeemed, we at last will join in the everlasting song which does not end, and which grows only richer and sweeter for all eternity.

—

Father in heaven, what a moment it was, and is, and will be, as your Son takes his seat on the throne of the universe. Our own brother. A member of our own race. And our God, in this one spectacular man, our Savior, Jesus Christ. We do indeed gladly bow with all nations, with men and women from all times and places, throughout history and around the world, and declare your Son, our King, to be Lord of all. Bring our lives ever more in stride with his reign. Make us increasingly worthy, by the power of your Spirit, of such a Sovereign. In Jesus' majestic name we pray. Amen.

Scripture reading: Hebrews 1:1-9

22. HIS SCARS WILL NEVER FADE

The Wounds Christ Took to Heaven

"Put your finger here, and see my hands;
and put out your hand, and place it in my side.
Do not disbelieve, but believe."
—John 20:27

We know precious few details about Jesus' resurrection body.

It was the same body in which he died, and yet it was not only restored to life but changed. He was still human, but now glorified. What was sown perishable was raised imperishable (1 Corinthians 15:42). He could pass through doors and walls (John 20:26), yet ate solid food (Luke 24:42-43). His "natural body," which died at Calvary, was raised and transformed into a "spiritual body" (1 Corinthians 15:44), new enough that those who knew him best didn't recognize him at first (Luke 24:16, 37; John 20:14; 21:4), but also, soon enough, knew it was indeed him (Luke 24:31; John 20:16, 20; 21:7).

Among the fascinating few details we have, one of the most intriguing is his scars.

"See My Hands"

The scars were the main way he confirmed to his disciples that it was truly him, in the same physical body, now risen and transformed. When Jesus first appeared to them, according to Luke, "they were startled and frightened and thought they saw a spirit" (Luke 24:37). Then he showed them the scars.

> *"'See my hands and my feet, that it is I myself. Touch me, and see. For a spirit does not have flesh and bones as you see that I have.' And when he had said this, he showed them his hands and his feet."*
> *(Luke 24:39-40)*

The apostle John reports that Jesus "showed them his hands and his side" (John 20:20) and includes the account of doubting Thomas, who "was not with them when Jesus came" (v 24). Thomas insisted that he see Jesus' scars for himself, to confirm it was in fact him. In pronounced patience, Jesus waited eight long days to answer Thomas's prayer; when he finally visited, he offered him the scars. "Put your finger here, and see my hands; and put out your hand, and place it in my side. Do not disbelieve, but believe" (v 27).

Treasure in the Scars

If Luke and John hadn't told us about the scars, we might assume that a glorified, resurrected body wouldn't have any. At first thought, scars seem like a surprising feature for perfected, new-world humanity. In fact, they might sound like a defect. Would we not expect that such an upgrade—from a perishable body designed for this world to an imperishable body designed for the next—would mean Jesus would no longer bear the marks of his suffering in this world?

We might expect that the Father would choose to remove the scars from his Son's eternal glorified flesh; but scars were God's idea to begin with. He made human skin to heal like this from significant injury. Some of our scars carry little meaning, but some have a lot to say, whether to our shame or to our honor. That Luke and John testify so plainly to Jesus' resurrection scars must mean they are not a defect but a glory. What is the treasure that awaits us for all eternity in the visible, glorious scars of Christ?

Behold His Hands and Side

First, Jesus' scars tell us that he knows our pain. He became fully human, "made like [us] in every respect" (Hebrews 2:17), so that he could suffer with us and for us as he carried our human sins to die in our place. His scars remind us that he knows human pain—and to the uttermost. Pastor and poet Edward Shillito (1872–1948), who witnessed the horrors of World War I, found comfort in the "Jesus of the Scars," who knew what it was like to suffer in human flesh:

> *The heavens frighten us; they are too calm;*
> *In all the universe we have no place.*
> *Our wounds are hurting us; where is the balm?*
> *Lord Jesus, by Thy Scars, we claim Thy grace.*

Because he chose to suffer for us, Jesus' scars also tell us of his love, and his Father's. "God shows his love for us in that while we were still sinners, Christ died for us" (Romans 5:8). Hymn-writer Matthew Bridges saw love in the scars and crowned him "the Lord of love" in his 1851 hymn:

> *Crown him the Lord of love!*
> *Behold his hands and side—*
> *Rich wounds, yet visible above,*
> *In beauty glorified.*

They are indeed *rich wounds*: scars that radiate glory, marks that demonstrate love, blemishes that were once the site of his agony and are now the balm for our healing. We marvel at his rich wounds, now the occasion for our life, our admiration, our praise.

The Lamb Who Was Slain

Finally, Jesus' scars—as healed wounds—forever tell us of our final victory in him. As the book of Revelation unfolds to us that ultimate triumph, it is our scarred Savior—the Lamb who was slain—who stands at the center of heaven and sits, with his Father, on the very throne of the universe (Revelation 7:9-10, 17; 22:1, 3).

From that first introduction as "a Lamb standing, as though it had been slain" (5:6), Jesus is referred to 27 more times as "the Lamb." Heaven's worshipers fall down before him, saying, "Worthy is the Lamb *who was slain!*" (v 12), and the book of life is said to be "the book of life of the Lamb *who was slain*" (13:8).

Far from forgetting his suffering and shed blood, it is a glory beyond compare that his people forever celebrate him as the Lamb who was slain, the Shepherd with the scars—in whose blood we have been washed (7:14), and by whose blood, once shed through his still-visible scars, we have conquered (12:11).

We will worship him forever with the beauty of his scars in view. They are no defect to the eyes of the redeemed but a glory beyond compare.

—

Father, we praise the Jesus of the scars. He took our flesh that he might be pierced through with nails and spear. And he rose again in triumph; and what glorious scars, what rich wounds, he now displays on his resurrection body! Father, we cling to his scars, and the good news they tell: that you are for us in Christ; that our sins have been covered, our debt has been paid, the path of life has been opened for us by the slain Lamb. Oh, what you do with scars! Oh, what glory can come from wounds! Restore our hope, and make our own wounds into echoes of Christ's, being beautified in his. In his wounded and glorified name we pray. Amen.

Scripture reading: Luke 24:36-43

Part 4

HIS PASSION WEEK

"When he entered Jerusalem,
the whole city was stirred up, saying,
'Who is this?'"
–Matthew 21:10

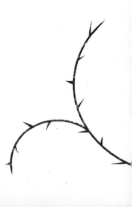

23. THE STRANGE AND WONDERFUL RIDE

Palm Sunday

"Hosanna to the Son of David!
Blessed is he who comes in the name of the Lord!
Hosanna in the highest!"
—Matthew 21:9

Having lingered over his life, the accomplishments of his death, and the glories of his new life on the other side of the grave, we come now to walk with Jesus, from Sunday to Sunday, through the eight most significant days in history.

We begin with palms. Branches are cut from trees, hands are raised in praise, and the most important figure enters the great city for his final week.

This unrecognized prince has a rightful claim to the throne of his people as the heir of their most celebrated king. And yet he rides in manifest humility, on the back of a donkey's colt—like no other ruler in the first century, or the twenty-first century, would dare stoop to do.

And this, of course, is not the extent of his meekness and lowliness. He will stoop yet further this holy week, and then further still when he is "raised up" to the lowest of all places, in the utter shame and ignominy of a brutal public execution, even death on a cross.

Glow of Palm Sunday

For now, the week begins with the strange and wonderful glow of Palm Sunday. The scene is radiant with the coming king, ushered into the great city by crowds stirred for the arrival of a veritable dignitary. "This is the prophet Jesus, from Nazareth of Galilee" (Matthew 21:11). In their excitement, the crowds "spread their cloaks on the road, and others cut branches from the trees and spread them on the road" (v 8), and so give "Palm Sunday" its name.

Joy shines this Sunday—a joy, as we now know, that anticipates a supernova of gladness coming on the following Sunday. In their thrill of hope, the crowds rehearse the praises of Psalm 118. Might this be, at long last, the great "Son of David," the promised royal rescuer, riding into the holy city to definitively save his people?

"Hosanna to the Son of David! Blessed is he who comes in the name of the Lord! Hosanna in the highest!" (Matthew 21:9). *Hosanna*—a Hebrew cry for rescue that came to be a declaration of adoration and delight—is the refrain for this triumphal entry.

Tinged with the Coming Pain

Still the light is tinged, even in the emotional highs of Palm Sunday. This is not yet his coronation at the right hand of God, seated on the throne of heaven. This is not the final triumph when heaven itself will descend and remake our fallen world—with all sorrow and pain, every tear of sadness, and every enduring rebel, banished to outer darkness.

No, even in the throes of the crowd's joy, the threatened authorities devolved toward a diabolical plot. The humble king healed the blind and the lame (v 14), and when the establishment saw "the wonderful things that he did ... they were indignant" (v 15). The burgeoning joy of the masses was the festering anger of the Jerusalem elite.

Joy Set Before the Man of Sorrows

Here on this Sunday we find, in microcosm, the joys and sorrows of the celebrated week ahead. This initial clash with the authorities anticipates the coming conspiracy, the traitor who will emerge, the fearful disciples who will flee, and the sheer demonic wickedness that will descend upon the city and culminate in Jesus' death by sundown Friday. And yet the joy of Palm Sunday forecasts the unrivaled euphoria to come on Easter morning.

The dark notes of Palm Sunday correspond to this unstoppably happy king being our "man of sorrows" (Isaiah 53:3). The joy of Palm Sunday corresponds to Jesus' own joy—his indestructible gladness, his willingness to come to Jerusalem and go even to the cross for the *joy* set before him (Hebrews 12:2). The one on whom is poured the oil of gladness without peer (Psalm 45:7) is the one who will be despised, rejected, and well acquainted with grief (Isaiah 53:3).

His Peculiar Glory

It is fitting on this strange and wonderful Sunday that the people would reach for Psalm 118:26 and cry out, "Blessed is he who comes in the name of the Lord!"

This psalm captures so well the curious glory of Palm Sunday. Just a breath before verse 26, the psalmist writes, "The stone that the builders rejected has become the cornerstone. This is the Lord's doing; it is marvelous in our eyes" (v 22-23).

The glory of Palm Sunday is not that the long-awaited king parades into town amid the pomp and flair of natural human expectation. This is not a king of unchallenged pedigree, born in a palace, nurtured by world-class tutors, surrounded by accomplished generals, trumpeting into the great city to conquer his foes and lay claim to his crown.

No, here is a Nazarene, a man from the backwater, purported to have been conceived in shame, a common laborer by trade, riding not on a noble steed but on the colt of an ass. He comes not to brandish his sword and demonstrate his quality to meet popular expectations, but to give his own neck to the knife and display his meekness in uncompromised sacrifice. He comes not to kill but to be killed; he comes accompanied not by generals and soldiers but by twelve very ordinary and unimpressive men, one of whom will betray him, another of whom will deny him, and all of whom will scatter when the real trouble begins.

Marvelous in Our Eyes

The long-awaited Messiah comes not in human glory, but a *peculiar*, a unique, glory—the glory of unconquerable strength in chosen weakness, the glory of indomitable joy in excruciating pain, the glory of the Lion of Judah giving himself for his people as the Lamb of God. He comes to be the stone which the builders will utterly reject on Friday, and which God himself will unveil as the very cornerstone on Sunday morning.

To the natural mind, it is confounding. A crucified hero is folly to some; a rejected Messiah is a stumbling block to others (1 Corinthians 1:23). But for those who have received the gift of true sight, it is marvelous in our eyes.

No human could plan it like this. This is indeed God's doing. Palm Sunday, and the Passion Week to follow, is no human creation and no happenstance of history. This bears the indelible fingerprints of the divine. This, at long last, marks the unveiling of the promised rescue, in all its strangeness and wonder.

Only a king on a donkey could truly save our souls, and fully satisfy them forever.

Father in heaven, we do marvel at the might and modesty of your Son. He is the King of the world, who rides in manifest humility, on the back of a donkey, like no other ruler. Hallelujah, what a Savior—strong enough to defeat the foe, gentle enough to not destroy his own. Draw us near to him now as we seek to walk with him for these eight days in Jerusalem from the palms to the pain, from the joys to the sorrows, from the cross to the empty tomb. In Jesus' name we pray. Amen.

Scripture reading: Matthew 21:1-11

24. JESUS' MOST CONTROVERSIAL CLAIM

Holy Monday

"I am the way, and the truth, and the life.
No one comes to the Father except through me."
–John 14:6

On Monday of his final week, Jesus wasn't afraid to stir up public controversy. He cleansed the temple and refused to rebuke the children's hosannas (Matthew 21:12-16). But, as throughout his life, it was the words he spoke—words which overturned the tables of his day and gave meaning to his actions—that were so controversial.

Of all the controversial claims Jesus made, this one in John 14:6, from his final week, may be more incendiary in our day than all the rest. In our pluralistic age, we read these as fighting words: a stand against the idea that any way and any truth will do. But have we missed another aspect of them—the comfort they brought the souls of his disciples as he prepared them for his death?

Comfort in the Chaos

His disciples are fearful, perhaps even beginning to panic. One of their own number just left as a traitor (John 13:21-30). Then Jesus announced that he himself would be leaving them (v 33). Now he informs them that Peter, chief among them, will deny him three times (v 38). Into this confusion and emerging fear,

Jesus speaks a consoling word in John 14:1-4.

The banner over all that follows is verse 1: "Let not your hearts be troubled" (also v 27). Jesus as "the way" is first about the comfort and peace and assurance of his followers. These are not primarily fighting words, but soul-quieting, heart-feeding truth. Comfort, not controversy.

Jesus is moving his disciples from being troubled to trusting. "Let not your hearts be troubled." That's the negative. Then the positive: "Believe in God; believe also in me." What is the great antidote he gives to being troubled, or being anxious or fearful? Faith.

And trusting Jesus is still the great antidote for fear today. But not just general trust. We need specifics—which he then provides. We could count them in different ways, but here are four.

1. God Has a Big House—and a Big Heart

The heart of what Jesus says will be re-expressed in John 16:7: "It is to your advantage that I go away." But first, he describes the wideness of his Father's provision. His house is not small.

> *"In my Father's house are many rooms. If it were not so, would I have told you that I go to prepare a place for you?" (14:2)*

God's house does not have only a few rooms, but *many*. That says something about his welcoming arms and generous hands. And about the fact that he can be trusted even in the present trouble.

And these are not just rooms in general; this is not just mercy in general. There is room "for you," there is mercy "for you." Jesus goes "to prepare a place for you." Do not be troubled; you will be in God's house! *I may be leaving,* Jesus says, *but I am going to secure for you the most important good imaginable—so good that it dwarfs every one of your fears, if you only had the eyes to see it and the heart to feel it.*

2. Jesus Will Take You There

Jesus has more details to give, and specific promises to make:

> *"And if I go and prepare a place for you, I will come again and will take you to myself, that where I am you may be also. And you know the way to where I am going." (v 3-4)*

Not only are the Father's heart and house ready for his chosen people, but Jesus himself will come back and take us there. He won't sit around waiting for the disciples to get to God on their own; he will come back and get them and bring them himself. And there is more.

3. Jesus Himself Will Be There

Maybe the two sweetest words in the passage are here: *to myself.* "I will come again and will take you to myself." This is the great consolation for troubled disciples. Jesus won't just get them to heaven, but he himself will be there. And the essence of that place will be communing with him: "… that where I am you may be also."

Here we find a shift from *place* to *person.* Not only is Jesus heading to heaven, to his Father's house, and not only will he himself come get us and bring us there, but heaven itself will be about knowing and enjoying Jesus. He will be there with us.

But Jesus did not go directly from this upper-room conversation to heaven. There was a pathway to walk.

4. Jesus Has Prepared the Place for You

Twice Jesus says, "I go to prepare a place for you" (v 2, 3). What does it mean that he "prepares" a place for his people?

Is heaven in disarray? Is God's house in shambles; will Jesus be the renovator?

There is a second "way" in this passage: not for us but for Jesus alone. And it's utterly unique to him. Where he goes next, after this upper-room conversation, is not first to heaven, but to death. "The way to where I am going" (v 4) is the way of the cross. Without Jesus taking this way on our behalf, there is no way for us to his Father.

"Preparing a place" doesn't mean construction in heaven, but crucifixion on earth.

Jesus Will Be Enough

What comfort, then, do we find in confessing Jesus as "the way"? What communion with him do we find in this truth for which we're often called to contend?

In John 14, Jesus speaks to his disciples in their confusion. In their uncertainty. In their anxiety and fears. And he comforts them by saying, in essence, "I will be enough for you." *You know the way already, because you know me. I am the way. I will be sufficient for you. You don't need to look elsewhere; you don't need to supplement me with anything else.*

> *You're disoriented, and I am the way.*
> *You're confused, and I am the truth.*
> *You're fearful, and I am the life.*

Knowing me is enough, and will be enough, he says. *Your search can end with me.*

His Glory, Our Joy

Jesus gets the glory of being "the way" (not "a way"), "the truth" (not just true), and "the life" (not just alive). We get the joy and peace and stability of having such a Lord and Savior and Treasure. "The way" is not, at its heart, belief in certain principles and execution of particular actions, but trusting and treasuring a living person. The heart of Christianity is not principles to live by, but a person to know and enjoy.

Jesus is the way. By all means, contend for this precious truth in the classroom, over coffee, and on the street; but don't miss its sweetness first in the depths of your own soul.

—

Father, we thank you for such a Lord as your Son, who not only turned over tables in the temple and silenced proud Pharisees with a word, but also paused, during the week of his own Passion, to speak words of comfort to his followers. So, too, we today want to receive his words of comfort, however controversial our unbelieving world makes them out to be. We embrace your Son as our way, since there is no other; the truth in a world of deception; our life in an age of sin and death. Comfort us, your anxious friends, in these days. In Jesus' precious name we pray. Amen.

Scripture reading: John 14:1-14

25. HE SEALED HIS FATE WITH A SONG

Holy Tuesday

"The LORD says to my Lord:
'Sit at my right hand, until
I make your enemies your footstool.'"
—Psalm 110:1

Now there was no turning back. With each passing hour, Jesus drew nearer to the lion's jaws. In just three days, he would be shamed and humiliated, tortured and executed. Each step toward Calvary met with increasing friction. How did he keep going? On the inside, he was singing.

As he walked that harrowing road, he was living out an ancient script with every act of faith. From Palm Sunday to Good Friday, the events of his final week often turned on quotations from the Psalms. On Tuesday, he drew one of the most important from its blessed scabbard, stumping the brightest minds of his day and silencing the loudest mouths. Now, their recourse would be to kill him.

David Called Him "Lord"

Psalm 110 was among the greatest riddles in Scripture, and yet it became the single most quoted Old Testament chapter in the New. It all began here on the Tuesday before Jesus died, when Jesus himself planted his foot on ground so holy and high that no one else dared tread there.

That Tuesday was intense. He had captured their attention with a donkey (Sunday) and a whip (Monday), and then fed them a full day of teaching (Tuesday), showing the Jerusalem elite what the Galileans had already seen: one who spoke with authority (Matthew 7:29; Mark 1:22). He didn't sidestep the inevitable conflict with the ruling powers but strode into their den and held his ground. When they questioned his authority (Matthew 21:23-27), he answered with three parables (21:28 – 22:14). Baffled as they were, he made it plain enough that he was directing his riddles against them. Having endured their challenges with patience (22:15-40), he then turned the tables with Psalm 110.

Now he asked the question: "What do you think about the Christ? Whose son is he?" As expected, they answered, "The son of David" (Matthew 22:42). Then came Psalm 110 and the zinger: "If then David calls [the Christ] Lord, how is he his son?" (Matthew 22:45). How could David's son be greater than David himself? Unless... But the dialogue was done. "No one was able to answer him a word, nor from that day did anyone dare to ask him any more questions" (v 46).

At God's Right Hand
Jesus would unsheathe the revelation of Psalm 110 again as he stood trial, late on Thursday night before the high priest. He remained silent at the parade of false witnesses (Matthew 26:59-63). Finally, the high priest erupted: "I adjure you by the living God, tell us if you are the Christ, the Son of God." Jesus then willingly sealed his fate, combining "Son of God" and Psalm 110 with the stunning, enigmatic "Son of Man" prophecy in Daniel 7:13:

*"You have said so. But I tell you, from now on you
will see the Son of Man seated at the right hand of
Power and coming on the clouds of heaven."*
(Matthew 26:64)

"Blasphemy," said the high priest (v 65), and off Jesus went to
be condemned, scourged, and crucified, with Psalm 110 fresh
in his mind. On the other side of the grave, his apostles would
follow their pioneer and unleash David's greatest oracle. Peter
preached Psalm 110 at Pentecost (Acts 2:33-36) and before
the high priest (Acts 5:31). Stephen's last words echoed Psalm
110 (Acts 7:55-56). Paul stepped onto that same holy ground
(Romans 8:34; Ephesians 1:20; Colossians 3:1). And what do
we say of Hebrews, which has Psalm 110 at its very heart,
referencing it *eight* times?

The great riddle of David's prophecy gave way to one of
the new covenant's great revelations. We might even sum-
marize the message of the New Testament like this: *Psalm
110 has come true.* Jesus is not only of David's line but is also
his Lord, seated now at the Father's right hand. But before
the great oracle fed the faith of the church, these words
nourished the faith of Jesus himself.

Nine Great Promises

What did Christ hear as he rehearsed Psalm 110 during the
week of his passion? How did David's great oracle give hope
to David's greater son?

Jesus would have tasted at least nine promises of his Father's provision in the seven short verses of the psalm. The
first is implicit: "... until I make your enemies your footstool"
(Psalm 110:1). God will do it; he will see to the victory. Then
eight explicit promises follow, seen in the eight repetitions of
will (in our English). How would these faith-feeding pledges
have landed on Jesus as he stared down death?

- Verse 1: I will defeat your enemies and put them under your feet, for your everlasting joy.
- Verse 3: I will work in your people's hearts so that they follow you gladly, not begrudgingly.
- Verse 3: I will refresh you continually and not leave you languishing.
- Verse 4: I am God and will not change my mind.
- Verse 5: I will defeat leaders who oppose you.
- Verse 6: I will repay unbelievers who threaten you.
- Verse 6: I will destroy those who mean harm against you.
- Verse 7: I will give you all you need to endure each step.
- Verse 7: I will preserve you in what is coming upon you.

His Father's Right Hand

As Jesus sang verse 1, he remembered who he was to his Father: his right-hand man. How emboldening to walk into that Holy Week knowing himself to be more than the "son of David," and even more than the "lord of David." He pursued Calvary's arduous path knowing something greater still: he was the Son of his Father, who would welcome him to his right hand.

What is the deepest meaning of Jesus being at his Father's *right hand?* This: the very power of God Almighty was for him. With unassailable sovereign muscle, the Father would execute perfect justice, in his perfect timing, for every detractor of his Son—all the way to the top, to "shatter kings" and "shatter chiefs" (v 5-6). Weak and vulnerable as this willing Lamb may have looked as he went to the slaughter, he had been *sent* by his Father, with a *mighty scepter* in his hand, to rule—to rule even from the cross in the midst of his enemies (v 2), and then forever on the throne of the universe.

Here, during the greatest week in the history of the world, the Son knew that he was destined for his Father's right hand, and he acted as his Father's right hand. He served as the ultimate human instrument through which God channels his power to remake the world.

—

Father, we praise your Son as the great fulfillment of those ancient enigmas in Psalm 110. He is both king and priest, both God and man, both son of David and Son of God: the one who could fulfill one of Scripture's most confusing passages and make it the most quoted. All of history, and the deepest longings of our heart, come together in the God-man, as he now reigns at your right hand, wielding as man your very power as God. We consecrate our souls to him afresh now as we walk with him through this climactic week. In his merciful and mighty name we pray. Amen.

Scripture reading: Psalm 110

26. ENTER THE TRAITOR

Spy Wednesday

*"Why was this ointment
not sold for three hundred denarii
and given to the poor?"*
–John 12:5

Wednesday went quietly. Too quietly.

With the previous three days awash in drama—Sunday's triumphal entry, Monday's temple cleansing, and Tuesday's tense exchanges, with the silencing word from Psalm 110—now Wednesday comes like the calm before the storm.

Out of sight, lurking in the shadows, evil is afoot. The church has long called this day "Spy Wednesday"; the dark conspiracy against Jesus races forward, not just from enemies outside, but now with a traitor from within. It is this day when the key pieces come together in the plot for the greatest sin in all of history—the murder of the Son of God.

The Plot Thickens

Jesus wakes just outside Jerusalem, in Bethany, where he has been staying at the home of Mary, Martha, and Lazarus (Matthew 21:17; Mark 11:12; John 12:1). His teaching again attracts a crowd in the temple. But now the Jewish leaders, silenced by Jesus the day before, will leave him be. Today they will avoid public confrontation and instead connive in private.

Caiaphas, the high priest, gathers to his private residence
the chief priests and Pharisees (Matthew 26:3; Luke 22:1-
2)—two competing groups, typically at odds, now bedfellows
in their ache to be rid of the Galilean. They scheme to kill
him, but don't yet have all the pieces in place. They fear the
approving masses, and don't want to stir up the assembled
hordes during Passover. The initial plan is to wait till after the
feast, unless some unforeseen opportunity emerges.

Enter the traitor.

A Miser and His Money

The Gospel accounts point to the same precipitating event:
the anointing at Bethany.

Jesus was approached by a woman—we learn from John
12:3 that it was Mary, the sister of Martha. She took " ex-
pensive ointment" and anointed Jesus. An objection comes
from the disciples—verse 4 says it was Judas: "Why was this
ointment not sold for three hundred denarii and given to
the poor?" (v 5). This was, after all, a very large sum—more
than a year's wages for a soldier or common laborer. It would
have been enough money to finance a family for more than
a year, and could have gone a long way for charity.

But Jesus doesn't share Judas's concerns. Here he finds extravagance in its rightful place. The kingdom he brings resists
mere utilitarian economics. He sees in Mary's "waste" a wor-
shiping impulse that goes beyond the rational, calculated, ef-
ficient use of earthly resources. For Mary, Jesus is worth every
shekel and more. The Anointed himself announces that what
she has done is "a beautiful thing" (Matthew 26:10).

Judas, on the other hand, is not convinced. Contrary
to appearances, his campaign for charity betrays a heart
teeming with greed. Judas's concern comes "not because he
cared about the poor, but because he was a thief, and having
charge of the moneybag he used to help himself to what

was put into it" (John 12:6). The traitor has long been on a trajectory of sin and hard-heartedness, but this extravagant anointing is the last straw.

In this heart in love with money, Satan finds a foothold—and what wickedness follows! Incensed about this "waste" of a year's wages, Judas goes to the chief priests and becomes just the window of opportunity the conspirators are looking for. This spy will lead them to Jesus at the opportune time and place, once the crowds have dispersed. And this greedy miser will do it for only thirty pieces of silver, which Exodus 21:32 establishes as the price of the life of a slave.

Why the Insult of Betrayal?

Why would God have the death of his Son play out like this? If Jesus truly is being "delivered up according to the definite plan and foreknowledge of God" (Acts 2:23), and his enemies are doing just as God's hand and plan "had predestined to take place" (4:28), why design it in this way, with one of his own disciples betraying him? Why add the insult of betrayal to the injury of the cross?

We find a clue when Jesus quotes Psalm 41:9 in forecasting Judas's defection: "He who ate my bread has lifted his heel against me" (John 13:18). King David knew the pain of being not just conspired against by his enemies but betrayed by his friend. So now the Son of David walks the same path in his agony. Here Judas turns on him. Soon Peter will deny him, and then the remaining ten will scatter.

From the beginning of his public ministry, the disciples have been at his side. They have learned from him, traveled with him, ministered with him, been his earthly companions, and comforted him as he walked this otherwise lonely road to Jerusalem.

But now, as Jesus' hour comes, he must bear this burden alone. The definitive work will be no team effort. The Anointed must go forward unaccompanied, as even his friends betray him, deny him, and disperse.

As Jesus lifts "loud cries and tears" (Hebrews 5:7) in the garden, the heartbreak of David in Psalm 41 ("Even my close friend...") is added to his near emotional breakdown. He is forsaken by his closest earthly associates, one of them even becoming a spy against him. But even this is not the bottom of his anguish. The depth comes in the cry of dereliction, uttered to the one he had called his Father: "My God, my God, why have you forsaken me?" (Matthew 27:46).

Even more remarkable than this depth of forsakenness is the height of love he will show. Greater love has no one than this: that he lay down his life for his friends, even when they have left him.

—

Father, we stand in awe of the achievement of your Son, our brother. He answered your call and loved us to the uttermost—and did it alone, as only he could. When it mattered most, his men betrayed him, denied him, and fled. And yet, Father, what faith, what obedience, what love, what a salvation! We do indeed treasure him and his work, and him in his work. Make our own lives grow in their echoes of his faith, obedience, and love. In the name of Jesus, our Lord and Savior, we pray. Amen.

Scripture reading: John 12:1-11

27. HIS HOUR HAD COME

Maundy Thursday

"The hour has come.
The Son of Man is betrayed into the hands of sinners."
—Mark 14:41

All Jesus' human life anticipated this hour. Every careful attempt at minding the messianic secret. Every emotional investment poured gladly into his disciples. Every glimpse of the ocean of his kindness as he healed the blind, the mute, the lame, and the demonized, and even raised the dead.

Now it is Thursday, and *the hour* has come. All history hinges on this hour. And it is utterly terrifying. Jesus must decide: will he turn to protect his own skin and soul, or will he stay the course and embrace his Father's perfect and painful will?

His dying began long before this hour, but now in Gethsemane, he must face the death to self that comes before the death at Calvary. Never has a soul been in such anguish. Never has a human been so undeserving of death. Never has anyone else faced such horror: to be made sin on behalf of others—to put himself forward in our place.

His Hour Has Come
Even as early as John 2, when Jesus turned water to wine, he knew, "My hour has not yet come" (John 2:4). But he

acknowledged that his hour *would* come. And it shaped him from the beginning.

When he went up to Jerusalem privately for the Feast of Booths, he knew, "My time has not yet come" (John 7:6). Once he began to teach publicly, it wasn't long before "they were seeking to arrest him, but no one laid a hand on him." Why was he spared? John explains: "Because his hour had not yet come" (v 30). Then again, in John 8, during this same appearance in the holy city, "he taught in the temple; but no one arrested him." Again John cites the reason for his invincibility, for now: "Because his hour had not yet come" (v 20).

But when Jesus finally came to this grave and prescient Passover week, he knew that, at long last...

> *"The hour has come for the Son of Man to be glorified. Truly, truly, I say to you, unless a grain of wheat falls into the earth and dies, it remains alone; but if it dies, it bears much fruit." (12:23-24)*

When Jesus reclined with his disciples in the upper room, he knew this was the hour (13:1). As he began his magnificent high-priestly prayer that Thursday night, he prayed, "Father, the hour has come; glorify your Son that the Son may glorify you" (17:1).

Why "Maundy"?
In the English-speaking church, we have come to call this gut-wrenching night "Maundy Thursday." Scholars suspect that the word *maundy* comes from the Latin *mandatum*, meaning *command*. It's a reference to Jesus' charge to his disciples in that upper room, after washing their feet (13:1-20) and watching Judas depart (v 21-30):

"A new commandment I give to you, that you love one another: just as I have loved you, you also are to love one another. By this all people will know that you are my disciples, if you have love for one another." (v 34-35)

Calling it *Maundy* Thursday (Thursday of the Command) may give the wrong impression—that the accent falls on *our* love, not that of Jesus. The focus of this Holy Thursday, however, is not the fresh charge to the church ("love one another") but the unrepeatable act of her Bridegroom ("as I have loved you").

When Jesus said, on that first Maundy Thursday, "as I have loved you," he was not mainly referring to his washing of the disciples' feet. He was looking forward to what the foot-washing foreshadowed—to his own death the next day and the ultimate sacrifice he would make to rescue them. Their sin, and ours, justly deserved the omnipotent wrath of God. Jesus' demonstration of his love for us would require far more than foot-washing. And even more than mere physical death.

Anguish in the Garden

When Jesus finished praying in the upper room, "he went out with his disciples across the brook Kidron, where there was a garden, which he and his disciples entered" (18:1). His hour had come, and this would be the garden of his agony.

His hour of literally excruciating suffering to come at Calvary would be preceded by emotional and spiritual agony past understanding. Here in the garden, he must make the final choice to subject himself to hell itself. He must embrace the pain, not just endure it. He must choose the nails and the darkness. He must step forward to receive his Father's holy wrath. He must welcome his hour.

If there ever was a holy panic, this was it. He began to be "greatly distressed and troubled" (Mark 14:33). Fully human, he confessed, "My soul is very sorrowful, even to death" (34). "Being in agony" (Luke 22:44), he fell to the ground and prayed that "if it were possible, the hour might pass from him" (Mark 14:35).

So great was his torment that "his sweat became like great drops of blood falling down to the ground" (Luke 22:44). He offered "loud cries and tears" (Hebrews 5:7). As he hung by a thread, "there appeared to him an angel from heaven, strengthening him" (Luke 22:43).

Anguish, for Joy

He knew that hell itself was coming. How then could he embrace it in all its horror?

Earlier that very night, he had told his men what his hour would mean: *anguish, for joy.*

> *"When a woman is giving birth, she has sorrow because her hour has come, but when she has delivered the baby, she no longer remembers the anguish, for joy that a human being has been born into the world." (John 16:21)*

In all the terror and torment, in all his sorrow and distress, he chose the cross because he tasted the joy to come. Isaiah had prophesied, "Out of the anguish of his soul he shall see and be satisfied" (Isaiah 53:11). Duty alone could not carry this hour. "For the joy that was set before him [he] endured the cross" (Hebrews 12:2).

At last, he resolved, "Not my will, but yours, be done" (Luke 22:42). He would obey his Father's command.

Never Again

Never before had a human heart, mind, and will faced what Jesus did in that garden. And never again will God require it. His Son's trip into Gethsemane was utterly different than any garden of anguish into which God might lead us.

Those who hate God will soon enough stand unshielded to face his omnipotent, righteous wrath. But they will never do so on another's behalf. And they will never do so for the joy set before them, or out of love for the Father and his people.

Never again will God walk one of his children through this garden of the shadow of death. We might indeed give our own lives in this world to save others here, but we cannot choose God's wrath in place of another's sin. What Jesus did on that Thursday evening is unique.

And yet this is Thursday of the Command: "*Just as I have loved you*, you also are to love one another."

Joy to Echo Such Love

Having been loved like this, how can we not love one another? How can we not, as the beneficiaries of Christ's irreplaceable sacrifice, ache to empty our own selves for another's good? Having tasted such fullness from him, how can we not gladly pour ourselves out to meet the needs of others?

Yes, we will love, as he commanded. But Maundy Thursday does not turn on our love. This is a night to marvel at what Jesus embraced for us. To be astounded at the uniqueness of his sacrificial love. To wonder that while we were still sinners, Christ died for us (Romans 5:8). "In this is love, not that we have loved God but that he loved us and sent his Son to be the propitiation for our sins" (1 John 4:10).

On Maundy Thursday, we don't mainly shoulder up to the charge to love others. We fall awestruck to our knees, face to the floor, and say:

For me it was in the garden
He prayed: "Not my will, but thine."
He had no tears for his own griefs,
But sweat drops of blood for mine.
How marvelous! How wonderful!
And my song shall ever be:
How marvelous! How wonderful!
Is my Savior's love for me!
("I Stand Amazed," Charles H. Gabriel)

—

Father in heaven, we gladly confess that our life, our all, turns not on our own love but on Christ's. Greater love has no one than him. So, Father, we do want to love others well. We do ask for your help, acknowledging that the grace to love well is buried deep in the stores of Calvary's love. Make us more like your Son. Help our love and lives to echo his. Help us to marvel at his Maundy Thursday obedience, as he faced the death to self that came before his death on the cross. In Jesus' name we pray. Amen.

Scripture reading: Mark 14:32-42

28. WHY WE CALL THE WORST DAY "GOOD"

Good Friday

"As for you, you meant evil against me,
but God meant it for good."
—Genesis 50:20

It was the single most horrible day in the history of the world.

No incident has ever been more tragic, and no future event will ever match it. No surprise attack, no political assassination, no financial collapse, no military invasion, no atomic detonation or nuclear warfare, no cataclysmic act of terrorism, no large-scale famine or disease—not even slave trading, ethnic cleansing, or decades-long religious warring can eclipse the darkness of that day.

No suffering has ever been so unfitting. No human has ever been so unjustly treated, because no other human has ever been so worthy of admiration and praise. No one else has ever lived without sin. No other human has ever been God himself. No horror surpasses what transpired on a hill outside Jerusalem almost two millennia ago.

And yet we call it *Good* Friday.

What Man Meant for Evil

For Jesus, that most horrible of days dawned in Roman custody at the governor's headquarters. His own people had turned him over to the oppressive empire. The thread that held the Jewish nation together was its pining for a promised ruler in the line of their beloved King David. Both David himself, and the prophets who came before and after him, pointed the people to an even greater king who was to come. Yet when he finally came, his people—the very nation that ordered its collective life around waiting for him—did not see him for who he was. They rejected their own Messiah.

In his own day, David had seen pagans plot against him as God's anointed one. "Why do the nations rage and the peoples plot in vain? The kings of the earth set themselves, and the rulers take counsel together, against the LORD and against his Anointed" (Psalm 2:1-2). But now David's words had come true of his greater descendant, as Jesus' own people turned on him to hand him over to Rome.

Judas Meant It for Evil

Judas wasn't the first to plot against Jesus, but he was the first to "deliver him over" (Matthew 26:15)—the language of responsibility which the Gospels repeat again and again.

The schemes against Jesus began long before Judas realized money might be made available to a mole. What began with maneuvering to entangle Jesus in his words (Matthew 22:15) soon devolved into a conspiracy to put him to death (26:4). And Judas's love for money made him a strategic first domino to fall in delivering Jesus to death.

Jesus had seen it coming. He told his disciples ahead of time, "See, we are going up to Jerusalem. And the Son of Man will be *delivered over* to the chief priests and scribes" (Matthew 20:18). At first the traitor was nameless. Now he emerged from Jesus' own inner circle of twelve. One of Jesus' close friends would turn on him (Psalm 41:9), and for the mere price of a slave (Zechariah 11:12-13): thirty filthy pieces of silver.

The Jewish Leaders Meant It for Evil

But Judas didn't act alone. Jesus himself had foretold that "the chief priests and scribes" would "condemn him to death and *deliver him over* to the Gentiles to be mocked and flogged and crucified" (Matthew 20:18-19). And it unfolded according to plan. "The band of soldiers and their captain and *the officers of the Jews*" arrested him and delivered him to Pilate (John 18:12, 30). As Pilate would acknowledge to Jesus, "Your own nation and the chief priests have *delivered you over* to me" (John 18:35).

On the day when God's chosen Messiah was grossly and unjustly executed, the human agents of evil standing at the helm were the formal officers of God's chosen people. Fault would not be limited to them, but to them much had been given, and much would be required (Luke 12:48). Jesus, speaking to Pilate, was clear who deserved more blame: "He who *delivered me over* to you has the greater sin" (John 19:11).

Even Pilate could tell why the Jewish leaders had it in for Jesus: "He perceived that it was *out of envy* that the chief priests had delivered him up" (Mark 15:10). They saw Jesus winning favor with the people and quaked at the prospect of their own power waning (John 12:19). Jesus' rise to renown posed such a threat to their fragile sense of authority and their claim to privilege that liberal priests and conservative scribes crossed the aisle to work together.

Pilate Meant It for Evil

In a web of wickedness, the guilty parties served their complementary roles. The Jewish leaders drove the plan, Judas served as the catalyst, and Pilate too had his own part to play, however passive. He would try to cleanse the guilt from his conscience by publicly washing his hands of the whole affair, but he was not able get himself off the hook.

As the top-ranking Roman on site, he could have put an end to the injustice he saw unfolding in front of him. He knew it was evil. Both Luke and John record three clear instances of Pilate declaring, "I find no guilt in him" (Luke 23:14-15, 20, 22; John 18:38; 19:4, 6). In such a scenario, a righteous ruler would not only have vindicated the accused but seen to it that he was protected from subsequent harm from his accusers. Yet, ironically, finding no guilt in Jesus became the cause of Pilate's guilt, as he bowed to what seemed politically expedient in the moment.

First, Pilate tried to bargain. He offered to release either Jesus or a notorious criminal. But the people, incited by their leaders, called his bluff and demanded the release of the guilty one. Now Pilate was cornered. He washed his hands as a show, "released for them Barabbas, and having scourged Jesus, *delivered him* to be crucified" (Matthew 27:26; Mark 15:15). Pilate, no doubt, was less proactive and more reactive than the conspiring Jewish leaders; but when "he *delivered Jesus over* to their will" (Luke 23:25), he joined them in their wickedness.

The People Meant It for Evil

The rank and file played their part as well. They allowed themselves to be incited by their conniving officials. They called for the release of a man they knew was guilty in place of a man who was innocent. Rightly would the apostle Peter preach in Acts 3:13-15 as he addressed the people of Jerusalem:

> *"You delivered [Jesus] over and denied [him] in the presence of Pilate, when he had decided to release him. But you denied the Holy and Righteous One, and asked for a murderer to be granted to you, and you killed the Author of life, whom God raised from the dead."*

The early Christians in Jerusalem would pray, "Truly in this city there were gathered together against your holy servant Jesus, whom you anointed, both Herod and Pontius Pilate, along with the Gentiles *and the peoples of Israel*" (Acts 4:27). Herod and the Romans are not clean either. In the end, in a surprising turn, Jews and Gentiles worked together to kill the Author of life.

And soon enough we come to find that it's not only Judas, Pilate, the leaders, and the people who are implicated. We see our own sin, even as we see through the blackness of this Friday to the light of God's goodness: *we delivered him over.* "Christ died for our sins" (1 Corinthians 15:3). Jesus was "delivered up *for our trespasses*" (Romans 4:25). He "gave himself *for our sins*" (Galatians 1:4). "He himself bore *our sins* in his body on the tree" (1 Peter 2:24).

Yet what sinners meant for evil, God meant for good.

God Meant It for Good

God was at work, doing his greatest good in our most horrible evil. Over and in and beneath the spiraling evil of Judas, the Jewish leaders, Pilate, the people, and all forgiven sinners, God's hand is steady; he is never to blame for evil but ever working it for our final good. As Peter would soon preach, Jesus was "delivered up according to the definite plan and foreknowledge of God" (Acts 2:23). And as the early Christians would pray, "Herod and Pontius Pilate, along with the Gentiles and the peoples of Israel, [did] whatever your hand and your plan had predestined to take place" (Acts 4:27-28).

What man meant for evil, God meant for good. Those were Joseph's words first (Genesis 50:20). Never has his banner flown so truly as it did on the day Jesus died. And if this day, of all days, bears not only the fingerprints of sinners for evil but also the imprint of the sovereign hand of God for good, how can we not fly Joseph's banner over the great tragedies and horrors of our own lives? Since God himself "did not spare his own Son but *gave him up* for us all, how will he not with him graciously give us all things" for our everlasting good (Romans 8:32)?

God wrote "good" on the single worst day in the history of the world. And there is not one day—or week, month, year, or lifetime of suffering—not one trauma, not one loss, not one pain over which God cannot write *good* for you in Christ Jesus.

Satan and sinful humanity meant that Friday for evil, but God meant it for good, and so we call it Good Friday.

—

Father in heaven, what wonders you worked on that singularly horrible and tragic day. Your own Son, God in human flesh, was slaughtered, in the single worst act of injustice ever perpetrated. And yet what a good Friday: the day Jesus bore the penalty for our sins, the day he gave himself to be delivered over to death, that we might be spared eternal death and receive eternal life! O Father, on this horrible and good day you have taught us so much about our every day. For your own children, beloved and called according to your purposes, you work for our everlasting good what sinners mean for evil. Give us the grace to fly the flag of Good Friday, the standard of the cross, over each day and each pain and trial we face. In Jesus' good name we pray. Amen.

Scripture reading: Mark 15:21-32

29. THEY DID NOT BREAK HIS LEGS

Holy Saturday

"When they came to Jesus
and saw that he was already dead,
they did not break his legs."
–John 19:33

It was only 24 hours, like every other day. After the long night, the sun came up, patiently ran its course across the sky, and disappeared. Night came again. But to the disciples and close friends of Jesus, as they replayed the shock and horror of the previous day over and over, it must have felt like the longest day in the history of the world.

On that insufferably long Saturday, what particular moments might they have grieved over most? Did they remember the whip, the crown of thorns, the anguish on the faces of every sympathetic observer? Did they rehearse the words Jesus had spoken—in torment, giving grace to his mother, grace to a criminal, grace to his revilers, grace to his enemies? Did they reflect on the spear that had pierced his side, confirming once and for all that their Messiah was dead?

And yet, in their utter devastation, as spasms of grief came in waves, did they have it in them to even wonder about the surprising, almost unnerving way his dead body came down from the cross? Might they have even dared to hold on to a tiny, almost invisible ray of hope hidden in six surprising words? As the apostle John writes, "They did not break his legs" (John 19:33).

Smash the Legs

The Gospel of John tells us of the unusual circumstances surrounding the removal of the bodies from the crosses that Friday. The Sabbath of the Passover was the next day ("That Sabbath was a high day," John 19:31). This presented a problem. As D.A. Carson explains:

> *The normal Roman practice was to leave crucified men and women on the cross until they died—and this could take days—and then leave their rotting bodies hanging there to be devoured by vultures. If there were some reason to hasten their deaths, the soldiers would smash the legs of the victim with an iron mallet (a practice called, in Latin, crurifragium). Quite apart from the shock and additional loss of blood, this step prevented the victim from pushing with his legs to keep his chest cavity open. Strength in the arms was soon insufficient, and asphyxia followed.*
>
> *(The Gospel According to John, p 622)*

It was the Jewish leaders, John reports, who asked Pilate to have the legs broken so the dead men could be taken away before the high day (John 19:31). The Roman soldiers smashed the legs of the two criminals, but when they came to Jesus and "saw that he was already dead, they did not break his legs" (v 33).

They did not break his legs. Instead, they pierced his side with a spear, to confirm he was dead. And the apostle John saw the ray of hope—and peculiar glory—in this surprising turn of events. Whether he held onto that hope already on that Holy Saturday or only later reflected back on it, there was meaning in this utterly surprising providence.

Can you hear the song in the distance? In keeping his bones intact and unbroken, might God himself have been humming the ancient tune of Psalm 34, even on this darkest of Sabbaths?

> *"Many are the afflictions of the righteous,*
>   *but the* LORD *delivers him out of them all.*
> *He keeps all his bones;*
>   *not one of them is broken." (Psalm 34:19-20)*

Keeping the Bones

Today we no longer attach much symbolic significance to bones. We scratch our heads at God's pledge to "keep all his bones"—as if that were a comforting promise to one who has already died! But in the Bible, bones are often filled with the marrow of figurative meanings.

Perhaps no bones in Scripture are more famous than Joseph's. The book of Genesis ends with Joseph making the sons of Israel swear to bring up his bones from Egypt to the promised land when God delivers them (Genesis 50:25). When the nation made its exodus, the pledge was fulfilled:

> *"Moses took the bones of Joseph with him, for Joseph*
> *had made the sons of Israel solemnly swear, saying,*
> *'God will surely visit you, and you shall carry up my*
> *bones with you from here.'" (Exodus 13:19)*

The book of Joshua also ends with Joseph's bones, closing the arc: "As for the bones of Joseph, which the people of Israel brought up from Egypt, they buried them at Shechem, in the piece of land that Jacob bought" (Joshua 24:32).

In the New Testament, Hebrews celebrates Joseph's concern for his bones as a great act of faith: "By faith Joseph, at the end of his life, made mention of the exodus of the Israelites and gave directions concerning his bones" (Hebrews 11:22).

Just breaths before Joseph's bones are mentioned in Exodus 13, the people receive instructions about the Passover lamb and its bones, in Exodus 12: "It shall be eaten in one house; you shall not take any of the flesh outside the house, and *you shall not break any of its bones*" (Exodus 12:46; also Numbers 9:12). Why add this instruction to *not break the bones* of the sacrificial lamb? Something sacred, it seems, is in the bones.

Bones Back to Life

Centuries later, God would give his prophet Ezekiel a vision of a valley of dry bones. These are human bones—the final remaining part of bodies that once lived. The dry bones represent the lifelessness of God's people; and yet not all has been lost. Something remains, even in death: *the bones*. God tells Ezekiel to prophesy. When he does, flesh returns to the bones, breath returns to the restored bodies, and an army of God's people *rises from the dead.*

In other words, intact bones, kept bones, unbroken bones represent the hope of resurrection—that God, in his perfect timing, will reassemble the bones, and restore the flesh, and give breath, and bring dry bones back to full life with resurrection power.

God's keeping the bones of the righteous in Psalm 34:20, then, is a promise of resurrection, of new life on the other side of death. As Derek Kidner writes about the stunning claim of verse 19—that the Lord will deliver the righteous out of *all* his afflictions—this "sweeping affirmation ... urges the mind to look beyond death" (*Psalms 1–73*, p 141). God keeps the bones of his people in death, in order to restore them to new life.

Note well, the promise of resurrection does not mean a promise of no death. In fact, the promise of resurrection *assumes death*. You must first die to be brought back to life. Psalm 34:20 does not promise that the righteous man will not suffer in the flesh, and suffer to death. But it does promise that God will raise him. God will put him back together and give him flesh again and breath again. Affliction, even if it kills him, will not defeat the righteous man in the end. Which is not only figuratively true for Jesus, but literally. And a remarkable ray of resurrection hope.

Not One Bone Broken

The reason why Joseph made provision for his bones was that he believed God would raise him bodily back to life one day. And the reason why God instructed his people not to break the bones of the Passover lamb was that one day God would raise the true Lamb back to life after he had given himself to the slaughter for his people. So John 19:36 reports:

> *"These things took place that the Scripture might be fulfilled: 'Not one of his bones will be broken.'"*

When we see this deep meaning in unbroken bones, we come with John to that darkest and most terrible of hours, with the lifeless body of the Messiah nailed to the cross, and we find a startling first glimmer of hope. *They did not break his legs.* The soldier with the iron mallet pauses, seeing that Jesus is already dead. The one with the spear pierces his side and confirms it—*and the bones of Christ remain unbroken, intact, kept in the providential care of his Father, who will put them back together and raise him.*

Jesus will rise again. It's only a matter of time. Long though Holy Saturday may be, these unbroken bones are the turning point. Here is an invitation to the disciples to dare to hope, even as they wipe the streams of tears from their faces. God is watching over this righteous man, and he has kept his bones. He will raise them. And in Christ, he will raise ours too (Ephesians 2:5-6).

Darkest Days, Greatest Light

As God's covenant people in Christ, we make no pretense to be immune to fears, troubles, afflictions, or death. Yet in the most trying of times, and even in death itself, our God keeps hope alive. In Christ, he promises resurrection on the other side. And he will deliver his people—not in our preferred timing, but in his. Sometimes, it's only one day away.

If we only knew deep down, in our bones—in the midst of our afflictions, however severe—what a resounding rescue we have coming! How much more ready might we be to bear up under our momentary trials, including the darkest and longest of days.

—

O Father, how many rays of hope you hold out to us, if we only had the eyes to see! Give us such sight. Even at Calvary. Even on Holy Saturday. Even on the darkest of days and in the longest of seasons and the most difficult of lives. Father, give us resurrection hope. Give us trust in your goodness. Give us rest, and patience for your timing. We want to trust a hope in the darkest of times—because you have shown us your heart, your love, your purposes, your goodness, and your trustworthiness, even here in the most painful of delays. In Jesus' precious and powerful name we pray. Amen.

Scripture reading: John 19:28-37

30. THE TRIUMPH OF JOY

Easter Sunday

"He has risen; he is not here.
See the place where they laid him."
—Mark 16:6

T he first whispers among his disciples, that Sunday in
the holy city, were almost too good to be true. This
news was so unexpected, so stupendous, such a dramatic
reversal of the heartbreak and devastation of the previous
three days. This would take days to sink in. Weeks, even.

In some ways, it would take his disciples the rest of their
lives to grasp the impact of it. *He has risen.* Indeed, for all
eternity his people still will stand in awe of the love of God
on display in Christ's death, and the power of God bursting
forth in his resurrection.

Sheep Had Scattered
No one truly saw this coming except Jesus himself. He told
his disciples plainly that he would be killed and then rise
again (Mark 8:31; Matthew 17:22-23; Luke 9:22). He had
hinted at it as early as the first temple cleaning (John 2:19).
At his trial, some testified against him that he'd made such a
claim (Mark 14:58; Matthew 26:61; 27:63). Then there were
his references to "the sign of Jonah" (Matthew 12:39; 16:4)—
who rose again from the depths of the sea—and to the rejected one becoming the cornerstone (Matthew 21:42).

But as much as he'd done to prepare his disciples for this, a literal crucifixion was so contrary to their expectations that they had no meaningful way to bring it into their minds and hearts. It was "a stone of offense and a rock of stumbling" (Isaiah 8:14) for the long-awaited Messiah to go out like this. So, his men had abandoned their master in his most critical hour.

One of them had betrayed him. The chief of them had denied him three times. And after his death, the disciples dispersed. "Strike the shepherd, and the sheep will be scattered" (Zechariah 13:7). They locked their doors (John 20:19). Two even took to the road and were on their way out of Jerusalem (Luke 24:13).

When news came from the women who had been to the tomb, it seemed like sheer fantasy. "These words seemed to them an idle tale, and they did not believe them" (Luke 24:11). It was beyond their imagination—but not beyond God. Could such a dream become reality? Might there be, after all, some deep magic that could turn back time? Better, might there be a power magnanimous enough to bring in a whole new age—the age of resurrection—and triumph over the final enemy, death itself?

Seized with Astonishment

The initial report left them in shock. Mark tells us that the women "went out and fled from the tomb, for trembling and astonishment had seized them, and they said nothing to anyone, for they were afraid" (Mark 16:8). *Astonishment seized them.* Had the news been less spectacular, perhaps they would have celebrated right away. But this was far too big and too surprising to melt into immediate rejoicing. They were stunned. That's what Easter does to the human soul when we own up to the reality of its message. That's how explosive, how cataclysmic, how *world-shattering* it is that Jesus is alive. It is a joy too great for instant gratification. First there is utter astonishment. Then comes the mingling of fear with great joy, and then the freedom to rejoice and tell others (Matthew 28:8).

Sadness Comes Untrue

But what now of his passion? What of his excruciating agony at Golgotha? Yes, as C.S. Lewis said, the dawning of this resurrection age "will turn even that agony into a glory." Now joy has triumphed over sorrow. Day finally has dominion over night. Light has thrashed against the darkness and won. Christ, through death, has destroyed the one who had the power of death (Hebrews 2:14). Death is swallowed up in victory (1 Corinthians 15:54).

Easter has become our annual dress rehearsal for that great coming day when our perishable bodies will put on the imperishable. When the mortal will finally put on immortality. When we will join in the triumph song with the prophets and apostles:

> *"O death, where is your victory? O death, where is*
> *your sting?" (Hosea 13:14; 1 Corinthians 15:55)*

Just as rehearsing the details of Jesus' final days leading up to the cross prepares us for the fiery trials coming on us, so also Easter Sunday readies us for the triumph that will follow. Easter is our foretaste of glory divine.

Christ has been raised. Daylight is no longer fading to black, but night is awakening to the brightness. Darkness is not suffocating the sun, but light is chasing away the shadows. Sin is not winning, but death is swallowed up in victory.

More Than Conquerors

Even agony will turn to glory—but Easter doesn't suppress our pain. It doesn't minimize our loss. It bids our burdens stand as they are, in all their weight, with all their threats. And this risen Christ, with the brilliance of indestructible life in his eyes, says, *These too I will claim in the victory. These too will serve your joy. These too, even these, I can make an occasion for rejoicing. I have overcome, and you will more than conquer.*

Easter is not an occasion to repress whatever ails us and put on a happy face. Rather, the joy of Easter speaks tenderly to the pains that plague us. Whatever loss you lament, whatever burden weighs you down, Easter says, *It will not always be this way for you. The new age has begun. Jesus has risen, and the kingdom of the Messiah is here. He has conquered death and sin and hell. He is alive and on his throne. And he is putting your enemies—all your enemies—under his feet.*

Not only will he remedy what's wrong in your life, bring glorious order to the mess, and vanquish your foes; he will also make your pain, your grief, your loss, your burden, through the deep magic of resurrection, to be real ingredients in your everlasting joy. You will not only conquer this one day soon, but you will be more than a conqueror (Romans 8:37).

When he wipes away every tear, our faces will glisten more brilliantly than if we had never cried. Easter announces, in the voice of the risen Christ, "Your sorrow will turn into joy" (John 16:20) and "no one will take your joy from you" (v 22).

Easter says that the one who has conquered death has now made it the servant of our joy.

———

Father, you did it. You raised your Son, our Savior, from the dead. He has triumphed, and is triumphing, and will triumph. Open our ears to the voice of your risen Son and his promises to us—to turn our sorrow to joy, and to give us the joy no one can take from us. We submit our lives, our minds, our hearts, our all to our risen Lord. We marvel at his life, and what he accomplished in his death; we wonder at who he is for us now, in his risen life, reigning over all at your right hand. Thank you, Father, for Jesus. We worship you in him. We bow before our risen Lord, in awe, in glad submission, in the undaunted hope of resurrection, and entrust afresh our small lives to his great purposes and plans. In Jesus' risen and regal name we pray. Amen.

Scripture reading: Matthew 28:1-10

EPILOGUE:
JESUS, I MY CROSS
HAVE TAKEN

Hymn for the Crucified and Risen Life

"I believe; help my unbelief!"
—Mark 9:24

We might call it "singing above our heads." Indelible Grace, the Nashville group that recovers historic lyrics through new music, describes it as "singing in two minds." Part of us believes and deeply wants the kind of radical life we are called to as we respond to all Christ has done, while part of us knows we're not yet there.

We may hesitate over the plea in the climactic fourth stanza of Henry Francis Lyte's classic hymn, "Jesus, I My Cross Have Taken":

> *Go, then, earthly fame and treasure.*
> *Come disaster, scorn, and pain.*
> *In thy service, pain is pleasure.*
> *With thy favor, loss is gain.*

Do I really mean these words? In view of Jesus' life and death and resurrection, does my soul truly welcome disaster, scorn, and pain? Tender consciences may be reticent to sing along, not because the hymn is any more radical than the words of Jesus but precisely because the lyrics are so steeped in the call of Christ and the bracingly stark realities of the Scriptures.

Lyrics like these help us grow and stretch. They press us and extend us and shape us into what we should be—into what we are not yet, but want to be, with the help of God's grace. Worship forms us. This hymn, in particular, leads us in what it means to live in the light of Jesus' life, death, and triumph. It takes us on a journey from Jesus' initial call, to the hard yet joyful road of the Christian life, to a taste of the blissful repose awaiting us just over the horizon. These lines put the sweet ups and painful downs of life in this age in the context of God's overarching story, precious promises, and ever-present help. They make for a fitting conclusion to our 30-step journey admiring the rich wounds of Christ.

Follow Him

The hymn (printed in full on pages 183-184) begins with Jesus' radical call to follow him (Matthew 4:19; 8:22; 9:9). Jesus is not an accessory. He is a treasure worth selling all to gain (Matthew 13:44). Coming to him means clearing the ground of our lives and rebuilding all in light of him.

> *Jesus, I my cross have taken,*
> *All to leave and follow thee.*

Lyte takes his cue from the two main emphases in the New Testament texts on following Jesus. The first is *leaving all* to follow Christ—the call his first disciples answered. "They left everything and followed him" (Luke 5:11). "See, we have left everything and followed you" (Matthew 19:27; Mark 10:28; Luke 18:28). This is a call that is costly in the short term but abundantly rewarding in the end (Matthew 19:29; Mark 10:30).

The second is even more daunting: *taking up the cross.*

"Whoever does not take his cross and follow me is not worthy of me" (Matthew 10:38). "If anyone would come after me, let him deny himself and take up his cross and follow me" (Matthew 16:24). In the throes of rebellion against our Maker, unrepentant hearts hate the real Jesus. They take deadly aim at him, and our following him puts us in their sights. It's only a matter of time till we're under fire too. Following Jesus does not guarantee actual crucifixion, but it does require taking up the cross: a readiness to choose him over life without him, come what may.

Yet, again, the embrace of near-term loss comes with Jesus' great promise of gain. "For whoever would save his life will lose it, but whoever loses his life for my sake will find it" (Matthew 16:25). In taking up the cross and exposing ourselves to new dangers in this life, we are securing "that which is truly life" (1 Timothy 6:19).

Abandoned and Deceived

This mingling of loss and gain, of real danger and deeper delight, makes these lyrics so powerful as worship and as a means of formation. I am "destitute, despised, forsaken," but Christ is "my all," and God is "my own." In Christ, our heavenly condition is *rich*, even as we are struck with our own successive waves of earthly *wounds*.

In such joy, the second stanza braces us for the inevitable:

> *Let the world despise and leave me.*
> *They have left my Savior, too.*
> *Human hearts and looks deceive me.*
> *Thou art not, like them, untrue.*

We endure the deceptions of human hearts and looks by seeing the smile of Jesus. His pleasure readies us, and steadies us, for opposition:

Oh, while thou dost smile upon me,
God of wisdom, love, and might,
Foes may hate and friends disown me.
Show thy face, and all is bright.

So also in stanza three, fellow humans will "trouble and distress me." Hear the refrain of Psalm 107 (verses 6, 13, 19, and 28): "They cried to the Lord in their *trouble*, and he delivered them from their *distress*."

As life in this age presses us with trials, we endure with the Spirit's power, and in the process we sweeten the rest to come. Not only will "the sufferings of this present time" not compare to the glory that will be revealed to us (Romans 8:18), but the trials themselves will contribute to making our future all the better. "This light momentary affliction is *preparing for us* an eternal weight of glory beyond all comparison" (2 Corinthians 4:17). Not only do the obstacles of this age pose no final threat to heaven's bliss, but the obstacles, as we've seen in Good Friday and Easter Sunday, go to work for our increased joy now. Afflictions, endured in faith, produce for us a greater eternity. God's designs in the griefs he lovingly sifts into our lives are not for our harm but for our eternal good.

Pain as Pleasure, Loss as Gain

Stanza four is the climactic declaration. We have reckoned with inevitable earthly losses. Now we *welcome* them, with the couplet that is the key line, and very heart, of the whole hymn:

In thy service, pain is pleasure.
With thy favor, loss is gain.

This climactic verse then rests from these radical declarations and plunges into the deepest realities of divine comfort from Romans 8: God's sovereign and fatherly goodness (v 15, 28):

> *I have called thee Abba Father;*
> *I have stayed my heart on thee.*
> *Storms may howl, and clouds may gather;*
> *All must work for good to me.*

Armed by Faith, Winged by Prayer

With God as both Father and Sovereign, we enjoy a settled peace, even as our boat continues to be battered. Stanza five speaks of "joy to find in every station," and the assurance of coming to know our "full salvation," and "ris[ing] over sin and fear and care."

We have been invited into a life of trinitarian remembrance. "Think" of having the Spirit in us, the Father's smile on us, and the Son's death for us. The sufferings of this life, towering as they may feel, cannot hold a candle to the eternal blessedness of the Godhead that is being shared with us, and produced in us, by Christ through his Spirit. *What are our grounds for complaint?*

This finally gives way, in the sixth and final stanza, to basking in what lies ahead. Not only do heaven's eternal ages lie before us, but "God's own hand shall guide us there." And it will be "soon" (repeated) that our hope is transformed into "glad fruition," when we see him face to face.

Lyte in the Darkness

When we join Lyte and the psalmists and sing like this, "above our heads," we reconsecrate our lives in preparation for the various assaults of the world. We prepare our souls for the rhythms of pain and pleasure, loss and gain, grief and joy, in the overlap of this age and the age to come. We ready ourselves to suffer with Christ, upheld by Christ. We embrace afresh the essence of the Christian life, for now, as "sorrowful, yet always rejoicing" (2 Corinthians 6:10).

This hymn is not a disgruntled manifesto of complaint but a declaration of joy, of exquisite delights that the unregenerate soul never tastes. Yes, we lose. But how much more we gain. We gain heaven, all things, Christ's own comfort, and God himself. In the end, and for all eternity, this is the great legacy of the one who came to live and die and rise for us, for the joy set before him: in him, we gain. We gain Christ, and all things besides. Such is the glory of his rich wounds.

—

Father, we want to sing above our heads. How can we not? In rehearsing the life of your Son in our world, and the power and purposes of his sacrificial death for us, and the reality and victory of his resurrection and ascension and reign at your right hand, we cannot be content with our hearts and mouths and lives not singing. Make the life and death and risen life of Christ resonate in us and echo through us—to feed us, form us, energize us, comfort us. You are the God of exceedingly and abundantly more than we can ask or think, and nowhere do we see this more plainly, more beautifully, more convincingly, or more definitively than in the person of your Son. We admire him. We stand in awe of him. We sing of him. We worship him. In his crucified and risen name we pray. Amen.

JESUS, I my cross have taken,
  All to leave and follow thee;
Destitute, despised, forsaken,
Thou from hence my all shalt be.
Perish every fond ambition,
All I've sought or hoped or known;
Yet how rich is my condition:
God and heaven are still my own.

Let the world despise and leave me.
They have left my Savior, too.
Human hearts and looks deceive me.
Thou art not, like them, untrue.
And, while thou dost smile upon me,
God of wisdom, love, and might,
Foes may hate and friends disown me;
Show thy face, and all is bright.

Man may trouble and distress me.
'Twill but drive me to thy breast.
Life with trials hard may press me.
Heaven will bring me sweeter rest.
O 'tis not in grief to harm me
While thy love is left to me;
O 'twere not in joy to charm me,
Were that joy unmixed with thee.

Go, then, earthly fame and treasure;
Come, disaster, scorn, and pain.
In thy service, pain is pleasure;
With thy favor, loss is gain.

I have called thee Abba, Father;
I have stayed my heart on thee.
Storms may howl and clouds may gather;
All must work for good to me.

Soul, then know thy full salvation.
Rise o'er sin and fear and care.
Joy to find in every station,
Something still to do or bear.
Think what Spirit dwells within thee,
What a Father's smile is thine,
What a Savior died to win thee:
Child of heaven, canst thou repine?

Haste thee on from grace to glory,
Armed by faith and winged by prayer.
Heaven's eternal day's before thee;
God's own hand shall guide us there.
Soon shall close thy earthly mission.
Soon shall pass thy pilgrim days;
Hope soon change to glad fruition,
Faith to sight, and prayer to praise.

—Henry Francis Lyte (1793–1847)

THANKS

Three books on Jesus, saturated in Scripture, and encountered in a formative season of life, awakened me to the wonders of his person and work.

First was John Piper's *Seeing and Savoring Jesus Christ*. Its thirteen short meditations on the glories of Christ, plus the preface, made for a two-week daily devotional I read over and over again, stunned with the majesty and meekness of Christ. Then came Don Carson's *The Cross and Christian Ministry*, which put the work of Christ, and the gospel, at the conscious center.

Then, as my emerging love for Christology sought out more food, Donald Macleod's *The Person of Christ* was the next step I was looking for. Like the first two books, I read it over and over. Still today, I pull it off the shelf often, and always during Advent, to meditate on the wonders of Christ and savor the God-man as Christmas approaches. Thank you, John, Don, and Donald for shaping in me, through your writing, a fascination with Jesus that has endured now for two decades.

For fifteen years, I've had the privilege of working for and with John week in and week out, first at Bethlehem Baptist Church, now through the ministry of desiringGod. org. Thank you, John, and the Teaching Team, and Leadership Team, for encouraging me to write about Jesus and his work, and prompting me to answer when The Good Book Company called.

Thank you to Carl Laferton and Rachel Jones who asked me to follow the Advent meditations (*The Christmas We Didn't Expect*) with thirty more on the person and work of Christ, for Lent, Holy Week, and year round. Thank you, Katy Morgan, for your multifaceted skills as an editor, from the book's title, to the Scripture texts, to macro and micro edits and ideas. Thank you, Marco Silva, for putting your eagle eye and skill to the indexes.

Closer to home, I thank God for Cities Church, now seven years old, and our shared love of both Advent and Holy Week. I love walking through the Christian calendar every year with you people. And thank you to Megan and our four children in the Oikos Bibliou. Thanks for seeming excited that Daddy works on books.

Finally, the highest thanks and praise to Jesus, God-man, Messiah, alive, reigning at the right hand, King of the universe. There is, in Christ, as Jonathan Edwards wrote, an "admirable conjunction of diverse excellencies" like no other. We will sing his glories for all eternity. Our very best of words in service of his praise are lisps and stammers. He is indeed worthy.

GENERAL INDEX

SCRIPTURE INDEX

BIBLICAL | RELEVANT | ACCESSIBLE

At The Good Book Company, we are dedicated to helping Christians and local churches grow. We believe that God's growth process always starts with hearing clearly what he has said to us through his timeless word—the Bible.

Ever since we opened our doors in 1991, we have been striving to produce Bible-based resources that bring glory to God. We have grown to become an international provider of user-friendly resources to the Christian community, with believers of all backgrounds and denominations using our books, Bible studies, devotionals, evangelistic resources, and DVD-based courses.

We want to equip ordinary Christians to live for Christ day by day, and churches to grow in their knowledge of God, their love for one another, and the effectiveness of their outreach.

Call us for a discussion of your needs or visit one of our local websites for more information on the resources and services we provide.

Your friends at The Good Book Company

thegoodbook.com | thegoodbook.co.uk
thegoodbook.com.au | thegoodbook.co.nz
thegoodbook.co.in